Written by Juliana Foster
and Tracey Turner

Illustrated by Katy Jackson
and Amanda Enright

Edited by Bryony Jones
and Philippa Wingate

Design by Barbara Ward
Cover design by John Bigwood

Buster Books

First published in Great Britain in 2013 by Buster Books,
an imprint of Michael O'Mara Books Limited,
9 Lion Yard, Tremadoc Road, London SW4 7NQ

The material in this book was taken from two titles previously published by
Buster Books: *The Girls' Book* and *The Girls' Book 3*

www.busterbooks.co.uk

Buster Children's Books

@BusterBooks

A CIP catalogue record for this book is available from the British Library.

ISBN: 978-1-78055-195-1

2 4 6 8 10 9 7 5 3

Printed and bound in February 2014 by CPI Group (UK) Ltd, 108 Beddington Lane,
Croydon, CR0 4YY, United Kingdom.

Papers used by Buster Books are natural, recyclable products
made from wood grown in sustainable forests. The manufacturing processes
conform to the environmental regulations of the country of origin.

CONTENTS

NOTE TO READERS

The publisher and authors disclaim any liability for accidents or injuries that may occur as a result of the information given in this book.

To be the best at everything, you'll need to use your best common sense at all times, particularly when heat or sharp objects are involved.

Follow safety precautions and advice from responsible adults at all times. Always wear appropriate safety gear, stay within the law and local rules, and be considerate of other people.

How To Do The Perfect Handstand

Follow these top tips on performing handstands, and you'll be flipping upside down like a top-class gymnast in no time.

1. Find an area where the ground is flat and even, and where there are no items of furniture or other obstacles that could hurt you if you topple over. Grassy areas are good because the ground is softer.

2. Stand up straight and raise your arms above your head.

3. Swing your arms down toward the ground in front of you, bending your upper body as you do so.

4. When your hands touch the ground, you need to move your weight from your feet to your hands. Kick your feet upwards, one after the other. This is the trickiest part of the handstand – if you don't kick your legs up high enough, they'll fall back down to the ground, and if you kick them up too hard you'll flip over.

If you're finding it hard to get your legs to stay up, practise against a wall, or get a friend to catch your calves to steady you as you come up into the handstand.

5. Shift around on your hands a bit until you are nicely balanced. To help at first, keep your knees bent so that your feet hang over your head. Once you've practised this, try to straighten your legs as much as possible.

It might be best to wear shorts or trousers while you practise.

How To Decorate Your Nails

Every girl needs tantalizing talons. Here's how to wow with cool, customized nails for a very special occasion.

You Will Need:
- a bowl of warm, soapy water
- a nail brush
- nail clippers
- a nail file
- cotton buds
- nail varnish remover
- cotton wool balls
- a cocktail stick
- nail varnish in various colours including clear.

What You Do

1. Submerge your fingers in soapy water for ten minutes to clean the nails and soften your cuticles (the fine layer of skin that grows from the base of the nail). Gently brush the nails with a nail brush, then dry them thoroughly.

2. Trim each of your nails to the same length with nail clippers, then use a nail file to remove sharp edges. Make each nail a similar shape – choose between squares, ovals or 'squovals' (which means a straight top but rounded edges). After filing, give your nails a quick rinse and dry them again.

3. Now choose a bright colour of nail varnish – bold red or fuchsia pink work well. Roll the bottle of varnish between your palms to warm it up – this makes the varnish easier to apply.

4. Load the brush with a small amount of varnish, taking care to wipe off any excess on the inside of the bottle. Paint a stroke of colour down the middle of your nail first, then down each side to complete it. The fewer strokes you use the better.

Have some nail varnish remover and a cotton bud at the ready to remove minor mistakes.

5. When the first layer is completely dry, apply a second layer of varnish.

6. When this second coat is dry, take the cocktail stick and dip it in some nail varnish that is a pale colour to contrast with the varnish already painted on your nails – white or pale pink work well. Draw a simple design, such as a tiny flower formed from seven dots, or a simple

heart – there are some other design suggestions shown below. You need a very steady hand for this, and plenty of practice (you could practise on paper before you try your design on your nails). Reload your cocktail stick with varnish regularly.

7. When your nails are completely dry, apply a top coat of clear varnish to seal in your design.

To make your nail varnish dry faster, plunge your fingers into a bowl of ice water (this will NOT work under a running tap).

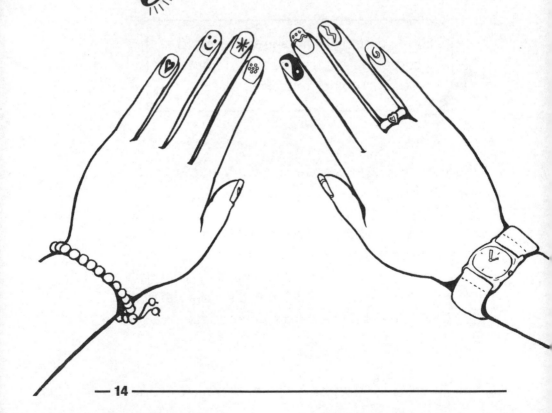

How To Whistle Really Loudly

A 'wolf' whistle is a good way to get someone's attention – or to really annoy them. Here's how to make this piercing sound:

1. Wash your hands. Place the tips of your thumb and index finger together to form an 0 shape.

2. Put these fingers into your mouth as far as the first joint. Point the nails of these fingers towards the middle of your tongue.

3. Close and tighten your lips around your fingers, so that air can only escape through the gap between them.

4. Press your tongue against the back of your bottom teeth.

5. Breathe out steadily, using your tongue to direct the air through the gap between your fingers. Pull down with your fingers pressing on your bottom lip.

6. Keep practising, moving your fingers, lips and tongue just a tiny bit at a time until you hear a whistle.

HOW TO TELL WHICH WAY IS NORTH

Telling which way is north is a useful skill that will impress family or friends when you are out and about. Here's how.

Handy In Both Hemispheres

You'll need a watch (one with hands, not the digital kind) and you'll also need to be able to see where the sun is, which doesn't necessarily mean it has to be a sunny day. (NEVER look directly at the sun, not even on a cloudy day, because you could seriously damage your eyes.)

Hold the watch flat in the palm of your hand and rotate it until the hour hand is pointing in the direction of the sun.

In the northern hemisphere, the sun is due south at midday. You can work out the north–south line by dividing the angle between the hour hand (the little hand pointing to the position of the sun) and the number 12 on the watch face.

In this example, it's three o'clock, so the north-south line runs halfway between the 1 and 2 on the watch face. This tells you that in the northern hemisphere, due south is halfway between the 1 and the 2, so due north is halfway between the 7 and the 8.

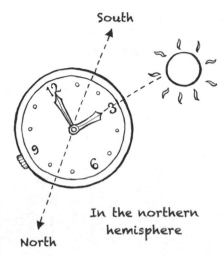

In the northern hemisphere

In the southern hemisphere, the sun is due north at midday, so in this example, due north will be between the 1 and the 2.

If you have a digital watch, check the time and then draw a clock face on a piece of paper. Mark the 12 and then draw in the hour hand in the position for the time shown on your digital watch.

A String Thing

If you don't have a watch at all, you can find north by putting a stick in the ground and measuring its shadow at different times of day.

You Will Need:
- a long, straight stick
- 2 medium-sized pebbles
- some level ground
- a piece of string
- a twig.

1. Place the stick in the ground and mark the tip of the stick's shadow in the morning with one pebble.

2. Draw a semi-circular line around the stick (to do this, tie a piece of string to the stick and a twig to the other end and mark the ground). The line should be the same distance away from the stick as the pebble.

3. The stick's shadow will get shorter as the time gets closer to 12 noon, and longer as the afternoon goes on. Wait until the stick's shadow touches the edge of the semi-circle again and mark the point with your second pebble.

4. As the sun moves across the sky from east to west the shadow from the stick will move in the opposite direction, from west to east. The line between your morning pebble and your evening pebble marks a line from west to east, so if you draw another line at a right angle to this, you will also have north and south.

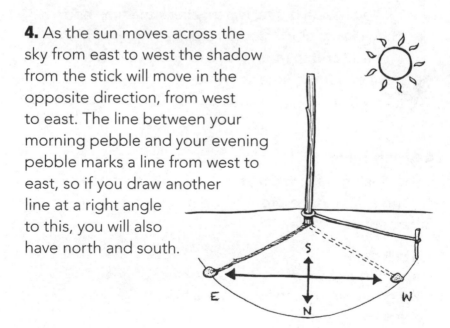

How To Write Your Name In Hieroglyphs

Hieroglyphic script was used by the ancient Egyptians. Some hieroglyphs represented whole words, others represented sounds or groups of sounds. It took Egyptian scribes years to learn how to write with them. Don't worry though, here's a simplified version of Egyptian hieroglyphs, with a symbol for each letter of the alphabet.

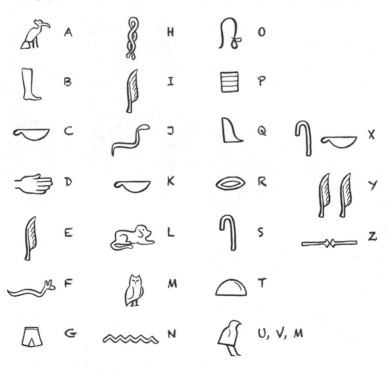

HOW TO DO
A FRENCH PLAIT

French plaits look great, but they can be quite tricky to do on yourself, so practise on a friend first. You need at least shoulder-length hair for the best results.

1. Brush the hair to get rid of any tangles, then separate a section of hair near the top of the head and divide it into three equal strands.

2. Cross the left strand over the middle strand, then do the same with the right strand, just like you would if you were doing a normal plait.

3. Now pick up some hair from directly beneath the strand which is now on the left. Add it to the left strand and cross this over the middle strand, as in step two. Repeat this with the right-hand strand.

4. Repeat this process, adding extra hair into each strand until all the loose hair has been added to the plait. Secure the end with a covered elastic band.

Voilà, a gorgeous French plait.

Once you've mastered the art of French plaiting, why not try splitting your hair with a central parting and wearing two plaits at the same time?

How To Make Friends With A Yeti

The Yeti is also known as the Abominable Snowman. Does the word 'abominable' worry you at all? Perhaps it should – especially bearing in mind that a Yeti is said to be three metres tall and weigh about 600 kilograms. However, if you're quite sure you want to be best mates with a large, hairy, mythical creature, here's some advice:

▸ First, find your Yeti. This will not be easy.
You need to travel to the Himalayan mountains
of Nepal and Tibet. Take plenty of warm clothes
– the Yeti has thick fur to keep him warm in
the snow.

▸ The Yeti is rarely seen, so it must be very shy.
Don't make any sudden moves, and try to look
friendly and approachable. Be patient – it may be
a long time before the Yeti trusts you.

▸ The Yeti is very hairy, so it may not be a good
companion for you if you suffer from pet allergies
– sudden sneezing may alarm it.

▸ Try tempting out your Yeti with food. Reports
agree that the Yeti is an ape-like creature, so
imagine what an ape might like to eat.

▸ Once you have charmed your Yeti, try interesting
it in winter sports such as snowboarding, skiing
or sledging. It may already be an expert, in which
case it could teach you some impressive tricks.

▸ Speaking to your Yeti could be a problem: it
may not speak English. In fact, it might be able
to communicate only in chimp-like grunts and
shrieks. You'll have to find other fun things to do
to make up for the lack of conversation. As well
as winter sports, try toasting marshmallows over a
campfire, star-gazing or flying kites.

HOW TO WORK SOME MAGIC

This simple trick will amaze any audience. They will see a coin lying beside a see-through plastic cup. You will cover the cup with a handkerchief and then move the cup over the coin. When you remove the handkerchief, the coin will have vanished into thin air. Here's how it's done.

Note. You will need to do steps **1** and **2** in advance.

You Will Need:
- 2 sheets of card
- a see-through plastic cup
- a handkerchief or other piece of fabric
- a coin
- a pen or pencil
- a pair of scissors
- glue.

What You Do
1. Take two sheets of stiff card. Place the cup upside down on one sheet and draw around it. Cut out the circle.

2. Dab glue all along the rim of the cup and place the circle of card on top of it. Wait until the glue has dried,

and then trim off the edges of the card if necessary, so that it fits exactly.

3. Put the second piece of card on the table and place the plastic cup on it, upside down.

4. Ask your audience for a coin. Place it beside the cup and tell them you will make it disappear. Cover the cup with a handkerchief and move it over the top of the coin. Say some impressive magic words and remove the handkerchief. The paper you glued to the cup will cover the coin and make it look as if it has vanished.

5. Cover the cup again with the handkerchief and move it away from the coin – the coin will reappear.

HOW TO GROW YOUR OWN TOMATOES

People say food tastes better when you have grown it yourself. Try growing some delicious cherry tomatoes. Grow them towards the end of April when winter is over.

1. You can buy cherry tomato seeds in packets, or you can scoop some out of a cherry tomato you are given for lunch. Rinse them in water and leave them to dry.

2. Fill empty yogurt pots with some compost. Push a tomato seed into the centre of each pot just below the surface of the compost and cover it. Water the compost lightly.

3. Label your pots clearly and leave them on a sunny windowsill. Check them every day, watering as needed so that the compost always feels moist when you touch it. Make sure you don't overwater it. After about a week you should see a tiny shoot appear.

4. After about four weeks, the shoots will have grown into tiny plants. Lift them out of the pots gently, taking as many roots as possible and taking care not to damage them. Transfer them to large flowerpots full of seed compost, gently firming them into position.

5. Keep checking and watering your tomato plants. After a few weeks, you should see some flowers appearing. These flowers will eventually fall off leaving tiny green tomatoes.

6. When your tomatoes are bright red and feel slightly squashy, they are ripe and ready to pick and eat.

> Don't store your tomatoes in the fridge
> – they'll taste better at
> room temperature.

HOW TO MAKE YOUR OWN PAPER

If you have any sheets of waste paper for recycling, why not have a go at making your own paper with it? Handmade paper will make a great greetings card or notelet.

You Will Need:
- waste paper (any kind will do, coloured or white – tissue paper, printer paper, wrapping paper, etc, but not newspaper)
- a mixing bowl
- water
- a blender
- a large washing-up bowl
- a wire coat hanger
- a pair of nylon tights (the kind you can see through)
- lots of newspaper.

What You Do
1. Tear your waste paper into small pieces and soak it in a bowl of water until it is soft.

2. Transfer the soaked paper into a blender and top up with water. Blend the mixture until there are no large pieces of paper left. Your mixture should be a thick pulp, like porridge, so use a bit of trial and error to get the right mixture of paper to water.

3. Fill the washing-up bowl with about four times as much water as you have pulp. Stir the pulp into the water in the washing-up bowl. At this point you can include some extra bits and pieces to make your paper individual. Here are some ideas:

- glitter
- dried flower petals
- pieces of coloured thread
- leaves
- seeds
- food colouring.

4. Bend the coat hanger into a rectangle – this wire frame will be the shape of your finished sheet of paper.

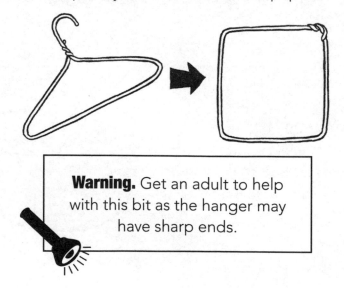

Warning. Get an adult to help with this bit as the hanger may have sharp ends.

5. Stretch one leg of the tights over your wire frame and tie the ends either side (these will act as your handles).

6. Lower your wire frame into the washing-up bowl, keeping it as flat as possible. Then carefully lift it out again, covered in pulp.

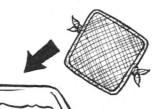

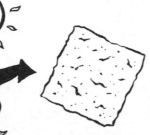

7. Lay the frame on some newspaper to thoroughly dry out – you can speed up the process by leaving it in a warm place such as an airing cupboard.

8. Once it's dry, gently peel the paper off the frame.

> Experiment with different types of paper, colours and added bits and pieces, for the best results.

How To Execute A High Dive

First, prepare yourself. Climb up to the high board at your local pool. At the beginning of the board, stand up straight with your hands by your sides. Walk towards the end of the board. As you reach the edge, turn around and stand with your back to the water.

1. It is essential to look completely calm and confident. Do NOT shake as if you are terrified that it is such a long way down.

2. Rise on to the the balls of your feet, and take tiny steps backwards until your heels are over the end of the board and your toes are on the very edge.

3. Launch yourself off. Stretch your arms above your head, with your thumbs touching. Then bend your knees, drop your arms down by your sides, and push down on the board. Jump up and away from the end of the board, swinging your arms forwards, upwards, and over your head as you jump.

Pike

As you rise, lift your legs so they are pointing straight upwards. Start bending your body forwards at the waist until you are folded in half. Reach your fingers towards your toes.

Layout

As soon as you've bent into the pike position, it's time to move out of it again.

Immediately start to straighten out your body. Your head should now be pointing towards the water. Bring your arms and hands forwards so they are stretched above your head.

Entrance

As you enter the water, your body must be completely straight, so that you make a minimal splash.

When you come to the surface, look cool, calm and collected. Swim to the edge of the pool and make a graceful exit.

HOW TO BE A
MATHS MAGICIAN

Ask your friends to try this simple sum. Read it out just as it appears below. Don't let your friends use a pencil and paper or a calculator – they must figure it out in their heads.

> ‣ Take 1000 and add 40 to it.
> ‣ Now add another 1000.
> ‣ Now add 30.
> ‣ Now add another 1000.
> ‣ Now add 20.
> ‣ Add another 1000.
> ‣ Finally, add 10.
> ‣ What's the total?

Your friends will probably say the answer is 5000. Congratulations, you are a maths magician, because this is the wrong answer. The right answer is 4100.

If your friends don't believe you, make them do the sum again using a calculator as you read the instructions aloud.

HOW TO READ TEA LEAVES

Some people claim to be able to see the future in the pattern of tea leaves left in a cup. Today, most people use teabags to make a cup of tea, but why not buy some loose leaf tea or cut open a tea bag, and have a go at predicting your own future?

Brewing Up The Future

1. Select a white cup to make your tea in – this will make it easier to see the tea leaves left over.

2. Brew your tea with the loose leaves, but don't use a tea strainer. Drink it, leaving only a little in the bottom of the cup.

3. Hold the cup in your left hand and swirl it around three times in a clockwise direction. Turn the cup upside down on a saucer to drain away the liquid. After seven seconds, turn the cup the right way up again.

4. Now turn the cup so the handle is pointing towards you. Look inside – what patterns do you see? A bird could mean freedom, and a shoe that you're about to go on a long journey. An elephant means that you should be patient, but good luck is coming your way, and a kite means that your wish will be granted.

Don't expect your predictions to come true every time. Maybe all you'll see are soggy tea leaves.

How To Cope If Zombies Attack

Fortunately zombies only exist in horror movies and won't be troubling you any time soon. But imagine if the dead really did come back to life – could you cope?

It is fairly easy to spot zombies – their flesh is a rotten green colour because they are decaying. They stumble around as if dazed or drunk, moaning and groaning. They will pursue you relentlessly and are hard to stop.

If you hear of a zombie invasion, you need to act fast. Zombies multiply very quickly. If a zombie bites or scratches someone, their victim will turn into a zombie too. Sadly there is no cure: once a zombie always a zombie. So it is vital to get to safety as quickly as possible.

Choose a secure place to hide out. First, check the news broadcasts regularly to find out which areas are zombie hotspots and which are less dangerous. You'll need plenty of food and water. A supermarket is an ideal base.

Lock all doors and windows, and pile heavy objects against them for extra security. Make sure you have an emergency exit if zombies do get into the building.

If you need to venture out for supplies, dress in bite-proof clothing at all times. Full biker's leathers are perfect.

If you find yourself in the middle of a crowd of walking dead, pretend to be one of them. Tilt your head to one side, dribble and moan. Hold your arms out in front of you and stare straight ahead. Try to limp slowly right through the pack. If they spot you, run for it. Zombies are slow-moving and stupid. If you change directions frequently, create diversions, such as overturning chairs, and scream, it will completely confuse them.

Zombies are hard to kill (mainly because they already dead). You can destroy them by cutting off their heads or crushing their brains. Some zombies will die if you burn their bodies, but individual body parts have been known to keep moving even after they have been cut off.

If you have no choice but to stand and fight a zombie, always check your body carefully for bite marks afterwards.

How To Flip A Pancake

Demonstrate your amazing chef skills by making and flipping a pancake. Here's how …

You Will Need:
- 125g plain flour
- 300ml milk
- an egg
- olive oil
- a tasty topping
- a fantastic flipping technique.

What You Do

1. Add the flour and milk to a mixing bowl.

2. Crack the egg and pour this into the bowl. Mix the ingredients together until the mixture (called 'batter') is smooth and has no lumps.

3. Pour about a teaspoonful of oil into a frying pan and heat.

Warning. Ask for help from an adult with this bit, as the oil needs to get quite hot.

Tilt the pan and move it in a circular motion so a thin layer of oil spreads out and covers the bottom of the pan. Turn down the heat to a medium setting.

4. Add two dessertspoonfuls of the batter mixture to the frying pan and tip the pan so that the mixture covers the base.

5. After about a minute's cooking time, check to see if the underside is cooked – lift the pan from the heat and give it a shake. If the pancake comes away from the bottom of the pan, it's time to flip.

6. Take the pan off the heat and tilt it away from you so that the pancake starts to slide (you might need to use both hands to hold the handle).

7. Now quickly pull the pan back towards you and upwards at the same time. Hopefully your pancake will flip up and over. Watch it as it does and be ready to move the pan up or down so that the pancake lands flat and not while it's twisting. If you're lucky, the pancake will flip 180°, ready to return to the heat and cook on the other side. If you're not lucky, it'll fall on the floor or stick to the ceiling.

Practice Makes Perfect
This mixture makes about a dozen or so pancakes, so you should manage to get it right by the time you're on to your second batch. When you do manage it, give yourself a huge round of applause.

Scoffing
The best part of pancake-making is eating them. Here are some delicious toppings to add to your pancakes:

Sweet Toppings:
- a squeeze of lemon juice and a sprinkle of sugar
- maple syrup and ice cream
- chocolate sauce
- puréed fruit (raspberries work especially well).

Savoury Toppings:
- sautéed mushrooms
- leeks or tomatoes
- baked beans
- grated cheese.

HOW TO MAKE A BIRD FEEDER

In the winter months it's hard for birds to find food. Give them a helping hand by hanging this easy-to-make feeder from a tree or balcony, and watch a dazzling variety of birds flock to your garden.

Find a large, dry pine cone that has opened out, rinse it under a tap and leave it to dry. When it's dry, spread peanut butter all over the cone with a spoon, making sure you fill all the crevices.

Spread some bird seeds on a flat surface and roll the pine cone around in them. Press down quite hard as you do so, so that the seeds stick to the peanut butter and don't fall off. Make sure all the peanut butter is covered with seeds.

Tie a long length of string to the stalk of the cone and hang it out of the reach of greedy cats.

How To Play Crazy Golf

Set up a mini crazy-golf course inside your house for a rainy-day sport that won't involve you and your friends getting wet at all. You'll need a fair bit of space, so make sure you're not going to be using rooms needed by other members of your family.

You Will Need:

- a golf club (an umbrella, a broom or a walking stick will work fine if you don't have the real thing)
- a sheet of paper
- a saucepan
- masking tape
- sticky tape

- anything that can act as a 'hazard ' – such as boxes, cardboard tubes, CD cases, books, silver baking foil, etc
- a small rubber ball (don't use a golf ball – they are too hard to use indoors).

What You Do

1. Work out a 'hole' – this is the route each player must follow. The route can start in one room and end in another. It should involve going around, under and over tables, chairs and sofas, and even down stairs. It can stretch through doorways, which the ball must pass through without touching the door or frame. It can include bouncing the ball off spots on the skirting board marked with masking tape.

> Do make sure you ask permission before sticking anything to the walls, skirting boards or furniture.

2. Mark the beginning of your route with a circle cut from paper, and mark the end of your route with a saucepan – the ball must be putted into this to finish.

3. Remove anything breakable from the areas of the house you're using.

4. Put in some 'hazards'. These could include:
- ▸ Cardboard tubes to knock the ball through

- ▸ Boxes that players have to bounce the ball off in a particular order

- ▸ Books or CD cases that the player must zigzag the ball between

- ▸ A long sheet of baking foil crinkled up, then laid out flat on the floor and stuck down with sticky tape – this makes it difficult to control the route of the ball.

- ▸ Boxes with 'gates' cut into the sides that players have to knock the ball through.

How To Play
1. Each player putts (gently hits) the ball around the course with the golf club, negotiating all the obstacles and hazards. A record is kept of how many times each player has to hit the ball before it finally ends up in the saucepan.

2. A penalty point is added if a player has to pick up the ball and move it because it's become trapped somewhere.

3. When everyone has completed the whole course, the number of hits and penalty points are added together for each player, and the player with the lowest number wins!

Creating a good course will involve some trial and error. When you think you've finished, give the course a trial run without scoring and see if anything needs to change – perhaps some elements of the course are just too difficult, while others are too easy.

HOW TO WIN A BET

Make a bet with your friends that they cannot fold a piece of paper in half more than seven times. It sounds easy, but no matter how big the piece of paper, it is impossible to do. Feel free to promise your friends anything if they succeed. Don't worry – they won't.

HOW TO GROW A CRYSTAL

Diamonds are a girl's best friend – but if you can't have diamonds, why not make a glittering crystal instead?

You Will Need:
- table salt
- warm tap water
- a jug
- a clean jam jar
- food colouring (in a colour of your choice)
- a length of cotton
- a small, clean pebble
- a pencil.

1. Make a saturated salt solution by dissolving normal table salt in a jug of warm water. You will know when the solution is saturated, because no more salt will dissolve and you'll see grains of salt at the bottom of the container.

2. Pour the solution into a clean jam jar, filling it about a third full. Keep the rest of the solution handy.

To create a coloured crystal you should add a few drops of food colouring to the salt solution.

3. Use a length of cotton to tie a small, clean pebble to a pencil. Suspend the pebble in the salt water, with a pencil over the mouth of the jar.

4. Leave your jar somewhere warm, such as on a sunny windowsill.

Allow the water to evaporate. Check it every few days and fill up the jar with the rest of the salt solution as necessary to keep the pebble covered.

5. As the salt solution evaporates, crystals will begin to form on the pebble. After a few weeks, you should have a lovely crystal.

How To Write An Award-Winning Haiku

Haiku is the name given to a type of poem from Japan. The word comes from the Japanese haikai no ku, meaning 'light verse'.

Haikus always have three lines. The first line of a haiku has five 'syllables'. Words are broken up into one or more sound chunks called syllables. For example, the word cat has one syllable, but croc – o – dile has three.

The first line of a haiku usually introduces the subject of the poem (what the haiku is about). The second line has seven syllables and often describes what the subject of the haiku is doing. The final line has five syllables and acts as a kind of punchline.

Here are two examples:

Sunlight on water
Dapples the riverbed where
Hides the spotted trout.

Black-and-white magpie
Bounces through broken branches,
Hungry for baubles.

HOW TO FIND
THE NORTH STAR

For thousands of years explorers have used the North Star to work out their direction and latitude (their position north or south of the Equator). Here's how to find the North Star in the night sky.

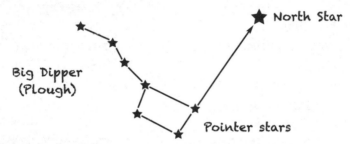

► First find the Big Dipper, which is also known as the Plough. This is the constellation which looks like a saucepan (remember that depending on where you are and what time of year it is, the Big Dipper could be upside down or on its side).

► Locate the two stars that form the edge of the 'pan' furthest away from the 'handle'. These stars are often called the 'pointer' stars because they point to the North Star.

► Draw an imaginary line through them and will lead you northwards to a large, bright star: the North Star.

HOW TO MAKE YOUR OWN SOAP

Decorative soaps are a lovely gift and they're easy to make yourself, which makes them even more special. Here is a simple method to make your own soaps in colours, scents and shapes designed by you.

You Will Need:

- a natural glycerine soap bar
- a cheese grater
- a jug you can put in the microwave
- food colouring in the colour of your choice
- a spoon
- essential oils of your choice
- soap moulds (you can buy these from a craft shop or use an ice-cube tray – these come in a variety of shapes and will make funky mini soaps).

What You Do

1. Use the grater to shred the soap into small pieces (get help from an adult with this as you don't want grated fingers). Put the pieces into a jug. Ask an adult to place the jug in the microwave and heat it on full power for about one minute.

2. Using an oven glove, remove the jug from the microwave. Stir a few drops of food colouring into the melted soap, until it looks a pretty colour.

3. Add a few drops of essential oil. Try lavender and tea tree, geranium and orange, orange and lemon, or lavender, geranium and bergamot.

4. Give your soap mixture another stir, then pour it into your moulds. It will set in about an hour and you can remove it from the mould.

Try making multi-coloured soaps. Pour a little of one colour into your mould, leave it to dry before adding a different coloured layer, then another colour on top of that. Alternatively you could add some glitter into your soap mixture before it sets.

HOW TO HIDE YOUR SECRET PAPERS

Every girl has at least one or two top-secret documents. Here's an easy way to keep them safe from prying eyes.

You Will Need:
- a large glass jar with a screw-on lid
- a toilet-roll tube
- a pair of scissors
- buttons, beads or sweets.

What You Do

1. Place the toilet-roll tube beside the jar and mark the height of the jar on the cardboard.

2. Cut across the roll width-ways about 2 centimetres below the mark you made.

3. Pop the roll in the glass jar. The top of it should be just below the top of the jar, so you can still screw the lid on.

4. Fill the space around the toilet roll with buttons, beads or sweets until the roll is hidden.

5. Slip your secret papers inside the toilet roll and replace the lid to keep your secrets safe.

How To Spot A Genius

Ask a friend to count the number of Fs in the following paragraph.

> FINISHED FILES ARE THE
> RESULT OF YEARS OF SCIENTIFIC
> STUDY COMBINED WITH THE
> EXPERIENCE OF YEARS.

There are six Fs in the sentence, but most people only count three. This is because many people's brains don't register that the word 'OF' contains an F.

Anyone who counts all six Fs on the first go is a genius.

How To Groom A Horse

Every horse lover knows that to keep their noble steed looking spick and span, they need to groom him before and after they saddle him up. Here's how to make your proud pony the smartest stallion in the stables.

1. Put a strap called a halter on the horse's head and tie it up with a lead rope so that it doesn't wander off while you're trying to groom it.

2. Start with a special tool called a curry comb to loosen up any dried-on dirt. Use mostly firm, circular motions, but you'll need a lighter touch on bony or sensitive areas like the legs or belly. Avoid the horse's face.

3. Use a body brush, which has thick, stiff bristles, to remove all the hair and dirt you've just dislodged. Use long sweeps, starting at the neck and sweeping in the direction the hair grows. Again, avoid the face.

4. Gently wipe the horse's eyes and nose with a wet sponge or soft cloth.

5. Use a mane comb to get tangles out of the mane and tail. Start at the bottom of the strands and comb downwards.

When you're combing out the tail, don't stand directly behind the horse. Stay slightly to one side to avoid being kicked.

6. Use a soft-bristled brush in sweeping strokes all over the horse to make its coat really shine.

7. Clean out the horse's hooves with a pick to remove any dirt or stones. Start at the heel and work up to the toe, avoiding the sensitive V-shaped area, which is called 'the frog'.

HOW TO MAKE BUTTERFLY CAKES

These little cakes are simple to make, tasty, pretty and perfect for a birthday party or a sleepover.

You Will Need:
(For The Cakes)
- 100g butter
- 100g caster sugar
- 2 eggs
- 100g self-raising flour
- a teaspoon of vanilla essence
- 12 cake cases.

(For The Icing)
- 50g butter
- 100g icing sugar.

(Optional Extras)
- hundreds and thousands
- small sweets
- crystalized flower petals
- edible silver balls
- food-colouring.

What You Do
1. Preheat the oven to 190°C (Gas Mark 5).

2. Cream the butter and sugar together (this means beating it with the back of a wooden spoon), until it's light in colour and fluffy. You will need plenty of elbow grease.

3. Beat the eggs together in a separate bowl, then gently stir them into the butter and sugar mixture, a little bit at a time.

4. Sift your flour a little at a time in to the mixture, stirring it in thoroughly each time. Make sure you do this gradually.

5. Add the vanilla essence and stir this in.

6. Place your paper cases in the dips of a cup-cake tin.

7. Spoon the mixture in to the paper cases, filling them half full. You should have enough mixture to make a dozen cakes.

8. Bake for 15 to 20 minutes, until the cakes look golden.

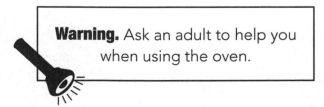

Warning. Ask an adult to help you when using the oven.

9. When they are cool enough to touch, lift your cakes out of the cup-cake tin. Leave them to cool completely on a wire rack.

10. Ask an adult to cut a circular section off the top of each cake with a sharp knife. Then cut the circles in half.

11. To prepare some icing, mix the butter and icing sugar together. Spread this on top of each cake in the hollow left by the circle you removed. Then push two halves of the top of the cake into the butter icing, rounded sides facing outwards, so they look like a pair of butterfly wings.

12. Decorate your butterfly cakes with any of the delicious optional extras you gathered. Gorgeous!

Why not add a drop or two of food colouring to the butter icing to introduce a splash of colour to your butterfly cakes?

How To Ice Skate

Do you dream of dazzling lights, sequins, and skates? Follow these top tips to become a champion on ice.

▸ Before you even set foot on an ice rink, make sure you have all the right gear. Ice is a seriously hard surface to fall over on and everyone takes a few tumbles at first. So wear knee and elbow pads, and thick gloves to protect yourself.

▸ Make sure that your skates fit well and don't rub your heels or squash your toes.

▸ When you first get on the ice, take some time to find your balance. If possible, go with a friend who already knows how to skate. Get her to hold you steady and pull you around the ice until you get used to the sensation.

▸ Keep your knees slightly bent forwards at all times to help with your balance – you shouldn't be able to see your toes. Your shoulders should be slightly forwards, in line with your knees.

▸ Try to relax your body, especially your knees. This will help you balance, plus if you fall over you are less likely to hurt yourself. If you do feel you are about to fall backwards, try to resist the temptation to put your arms out to stop yourself. A sore bottom is better than a broken wrist!

▸ To skate forwards, shift your weight over on to your left foot and push your right foot outwards in a diagonal stroke. Then repeat this transferring your weight to your right leg pushing out with your left foot. Move your body with the strokes. When you feel more confident, try to take longer strokes. With practice you will begin to be able to glide across the ice.

▸ The easiest way to stop is to place one foot behind you with the front point of that skate digging into the ice. Drag this back foot along the ice to slow yourself down until you stop.

How To Find Your Blind Spot

How is it possible to look right at something but not be able to see it, even with your eyes open? Read on to find out.

1. Place one hand over your left eye and hold this book in your right hand. Stare at the black circle below.

2. Gradually move the book closer and closer to your face, still staring at the circle.

3. When the book is a certain distance from your face, you will notice that the star will vanish. Bingo! You have found your blind spot.

A part of your eye called the retina is covered in cells that detect light. You have a blind spot because there is a bit of your retina that doesn't have any of these cells.

HOW TO PLAY MUSICAL CLOTHES

Play this game of 'Musical Clothes' – it's very similar to 'Musical Chairs', except when the game is over you end up looking very silly indeed.

What You Need

All you need is a bag full of old clothes in as many different sizes and types as you can find. The more crimes against fashion the better. Coats, hats, earmuffs, jumpers, T-shirts, bras, trousers, skirts, shorts and shoes – get your friends to bring a few items each.

How To Play

1. You need one volunteer to control the music, while everyone else sits in a circle.

2. When the music starts, pass the bag of clothes around the circle. When the music stops, the person holding the bag has to shut her eyes, rummage in the bag, pull out an item of clothing and put it on.

3. The music starts again, and the game continues until all the clothes in the bag have been used up.

4. At this point, the friend controlling the music gets to choose the winner – the person who looks silliest!

HOW TO MAKE A PAPER FLOWER

These paper flowers are simple to make, and look great added as decoration to wrapped gifts.

You Will Need:
- 4 sheets of coloured tissue paper about 15cm by 8cm
- scissors
- a length of thread.

What You Do

1. Lay the four sheets of tissue paper on top of one another. Fold them into a 'concertina' (by folding about 1 centimetre up then turning the tissue paper over and folding 1cm back, and so on).

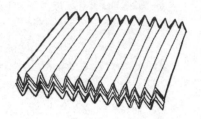

2. Use scissors to round off the straight edge at each end of your folded paper strip.

3. Squeeze the middle of the strip between your fingers, and tie it securely with cotton. Fan out each side.

4. Very carefully separate the four layers of tissue paper, and fluff them up to make a flower head.

HOW TO MAKE A CAMP IN THE WILDERNESS

So, your plane has crashed in the middle of nowhere and you need to keep yourself alive until help arrives. You can survive for much longer without food than without water, so finding water is your first priority. You need to find a spot to set up camp that is near a source of water, but not too near, as wild animals may gather there to drink.

> If you cannot find a good source of water, try collecting rainwater in a container, or gathering dew from leaves in the morning. Store it carefully so it doesn't evaporate.

You need to build a lean-to to keep you dry and protected from the sun or rain. Every lean-to requires a strong supporting structure. See if you can find a fallen tree, a natural cave or a big rock to build your lean-to against. Collect thick sticks and branches and prop them up at an angle along the tree trunk or rock face. Make sure the space under the line of sticks is long enough to cover your whole body when you lie underneath them.

Gather smaller branches and sticks, and use them to fill the gaps between the larger ones. Then heap leaves, grass, moss, ferns or whatever you can find over the sticks. This will keep some of the wind and rain out of your lean-to, and hopefully keep some of your body heat inside.

Collect together a large stack of dry wood to make a fire. You can also use bark or even dry animal dung. Make your fire at least ten paces from your lean-to, as you don't want the smoke to bother you, or the dry brush to catch fire.

To keep yourself extra warm at night, you could heat rocks on the fire and then bury them in the ground and sleep on top of them.

It is essential to keep your fire alight at all times and have a pile of damp leaves ready beside it. If you hear a plane or helicopter fly overhead, throw the leaves on top of the fire to create a plume of smoke that will attract attention.

When it comes to foraging for food, be careful. Don't be tempted by mushrooms – even experts sometimes find it hard to tell which ones are good to eat and which are poisonous. Berries can also be dangerous. As a general rule, most white or yellow berries are poisonous and most blue or black berries are not, but there are exceptions. Your best bet is to eat insects. It may sound disgusting, but they are nutritious and are not likely to be harmful.

It is better to stay in one place if you know someone will be looking for you.

HOW TO MAKE UP A ROPE ROUTINE

Skipping is a great way to keep fit, and it's fun, too. Master these complex routines and wow your friends.

Skipping Moves

First, practise these basic moves:

Backwards Jump: just turn the rope backwards instead of forwards.

Double Jump: jump up high and turn the rope twice before you land.

Hop-And-Skip Jump: land on your right foot, then on your left.

Crossover Jump: cross your arms in front of you as you jump the rope.

Slalom: land with your knees to the right, then with your knees to the left – as if you were skiing down a slalom slope.

Jumping Jill: land with your feet apart, then with your feet together.

Figure-Of-Eight Jump: move the rope in a figure-of-eight pattern while you stand still.

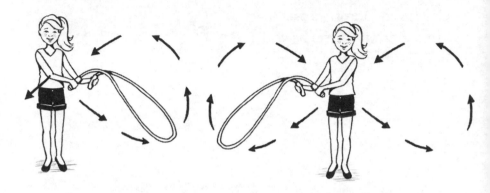

Balanced Jump: put your right hand under your right knee as you turn the rope – carry on skipping and land on your left leg. Then put your left hand under your left knee and land on your right leg.

Routines

Once you have mastered these basic moves, try putting them together in this routine:

▸ 5 double jumps

▸ 5 backwards jumps

▸ 10 hop-and-skip jumps

▸ 5 figure-of-eight jumps

▸ 2 crossover jumps

▸ 5 jumping Jills

▸ 2 balanced jumps.

Why not make up some jumps and routines of your own?

HOW TO PLAY 'WHAT'S IN THE BAG?'

Here is a ghoulish game called 'What's In The Bag?' that's perfect to play at a Halloween party or a spoooooky sleepover to freak out your friends. Any number of people can play.

You'll need to do a little bit of preparation in advance.

You Will Need:
- some opaque polythene bags (which means bags that you can't see through)
- peeled raw carrots
- peeled grapes
- cooked spaghetti
- mashed banana
- cottage cheese
- cooked rice.

Shortly before your guests arrive, put each item into a separate bag.

> It's a good idea to play this game at the beginning of your party, because your gross ingredients are best when fresh.

As soon as your guests arrive, get them to gather round. Set the scene with a scary story.

Tell them that, earlier on, you were passing a graveyard, when you noticed a strange-looking woman sitting in front of a huge cooking pot. She was muttering and throwing things into the pot. You asked her what ingredients she was using and she demanded that you guess by feeling them, not seeing them.

Tell your friends that you have bags containing each of the witch's horrible ingredients. Now it is their turn to identify what they are. Pass around the bags of different ingredients. Tell your friends to feel inside, but not to look.

They probably won't guess what is inside each bag so tell them these chilling ingredients:

- ▸ Fingers (carrots)
- ▸ Eyeballs (grapes)
- ▸ Maggots (rice)
- ▸ Worms (spaghetti)
- ▸ Bats' brains (cottage cheese)
- ▸ Frogs' innards (mashed banana).

How To Build The Best Sand Castles

Find a good spot. You need wet sand to build with, but don't pick somewhere too near the sea or your sand castle could get washed away.

Create a firm, flat surface for your sand castle by slapping the sand with the back of your spade and then smoothing it over.

Create the main body of your castle with buckets of sand. As you fill a bucket with sand, make sure it is tightly packed in. Tap the sides firmly and jiggle it around to get rid of any air pockets. When the sand reaches the top of the bucket, press it down firmly.

Build tall towers on top of your base structure by moulding wet sand into pancake shapes that are as thick as your thumb and layering them on top of each other.

Squeeze handfuls of wet sand to get rid of extra moisture and stack the clumps around your castle to build a wall. Keep adding to the clumps until your wall is as high as you want. The wall should get narrower towards the top to prevent it toppling over.

Add archways by carefully tunnelling through your wall at the base and then shaping the arches using a thin stick or even a plastic picnic knife.

As a finishing touch, dig a trench around your wall and fill it with water to make a moat for your castle.

Take a photo of your sand castle – quickly – before it gets washed away!

HOW TO MAKE YOUR OWN CHRISTMAS CRACKERS

Everyone loves pulling crackers at Christmas and groaning at the corny jokes. They're easy to make, and the best bit is that you get to choose what goes inside. Here's how to make one …

You Will Need:
- wrapping paper
- scissors
- 2 toilet roll tubes
- cracker snaps (available from most craft shops)
- glue or sticky tape
- ribbon
- goodies to go inside the crackers (see below).

Cracking Contents
- a slip of paper with a terrible joke on it (see page 78)
- a paper crown
- small pens, pencils or erasers
- sample-size sachets of shampoo, bubble bath or moisturiser – the kind that come free in magazines
- hair bands or clips
- wrapped sweets (if you're including chocolates, remember not to leave the finished cracker anywhere warm)
- a balloon
- glitter or confetti (to make a sparkly shower when you pull the cracker).

What You Do

1. Cut out a rectangle of wrapping paper – its length should be equal to two-and-a-half times the length of your toilet roll, and it should be wide enough to go around it one-and-a-half times. Place the rectangle on a flat surface, patterned-side down.

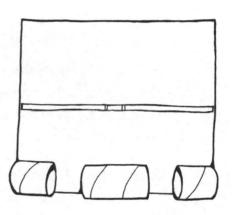

2. Cut one of the toilet roll tubes in half. Place the two halves either side of the whole roll with a 5 centimetre gap between them along one of the long edges of the wrapping paper, as shown. Place the cracker snap on the paper beside them.

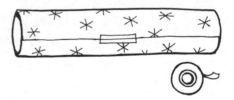

3. Roll the wrapping paper around the tubes and neatly glue or tape the join.

4. Carefully pinch the paper between one end of the tube and the half tube. Tie it with ribbon.

5. Put your goodies inside the open end of the cracker. Make sure your goodies aren't too heavy.

6. Carefully pinch the paper between the other end of the tube and the half tube to secure the goodies inside your cracker (and to stop anyone from peeking). Tie it with more ribbon.

Some Truly Awful Cracker Jokes
Here are some seasonal jokes to make you cringe. Pop them on a piece of paper and slip them into your crackers.

▸ Which of Santa's reindeer can jump higher than a house? They all can – houses can't jump.

▸ What's brown and creeps around the house? Mince spies.

▸ What happens if you eat Christmas decorations? You get tinsel-itus.

▸ What's a monkey's favourite Christmas song? Jungle Bells.

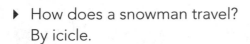 

▸ How does a snowman travel?
By icicle.

▸ What's Santa's favourite pizza?
One that's deep pan, crisp and even.

▸ On which side do turkeys have the most feathers?
On the outside.

▸ Where does Santa go after Christmas to recover?
An elf farm.

How To Persuade Your Parents To Get A Pet

Before you start your pet-purchase campaign, be sure that you really do want a pet and are prepared to take full responsibility for it.

▶ Think carefully about the kind of animal your household can accommodate and look after. You might be dying to own a pony, but if you live in a city it is probably not a great idea.

▶ Research as much as you can about the animal of your choice. The more knowledge you have, the easier it will be to convince your parents that you have really put some genuine thought into it.

▶ Before approaching your parents, make a list of all the possible objections they may have. Try to come up with reasonable answers to all of their concerns.

▶ Consider getting an after-school job that involves looking after animals. You could try dog-walking, helping out at your local stables, or volunteering at an animal shelter. This will help your parents to feel more confident of your ability to care for your proposed pet.

▸ If you have a friend who owns the kind of animal you want, invite her over to talk pet care to your parents.

▸ Start off by thinking small. If your parents are adamant that you can't have that puppy you long for, ask them to consider letting you have a smaller animal, such as a hamster or a goldfish. If you take good care of the small animal over a long period of time, they may reconsider buying you the puppy you really wanted. Alternatively, you may discover you and your fishy friend are completely happy, thank you.

Be persistent with your request, but always remain calm and polite. Tantrums and tears will only prove that you are not mature enough to look after a pet.

HOW TO MEASURE A TREE

You don't need to climb to the top branches trailing a very long tape measure to calculate the height of a tree. Here's an easy method that doesn't involve any scrambling through leaves or scrabbling up prickly branches.

You Will Need:
- a brightly coloured ribbon
- a tape measure
- a pencil
- oh, and a tree.

What You Do
1. With the tape measure, find a point on the trunk that is 1.5 metres from the base of the tree. Affix your ribbon around the trunk at at this point.

2. Walk away from the tree until you can see the whole tree and the marker.

3. Hold your pencil upright at arm's length, and close one eye. Line up the bottom of the tree with

the bottom of your pencil, and move your thumb nail up the pencil until it lines up with the marker on the trunk. The distance you have measured along your pencil is equivalent to 1.5 metres.

4. Count how many times this measure fits before you reach the top of the tree and multiply this number by 1.5.

For example, if your measure fits three times, the tree must be 3 x 1.5, which equals 4.5 metres tall.

How To Tame A Wild Horse

When attempting to deal with any animal, the best approach is to mimic their behaviour. So you need to get to know exactly how horses behave so you can copy their body language.

1. Horses have rough, dry patches called 'chestnuts' on the insides of their legs, just above the knee. Find a tame horse and carefully peel off the top layer of the chestnut. Rub the patch with your hands to mask your human scent. This will make it easier for you to approach the wild horse.

2. Approach the horse from the side. Horses' eyes are on the side of their heads, so they cannot see directly in front or behind. If the horse can sense you but can't see you, it will be spooked. Move slowly and steadily at all times.

3. Be very calm and very cautious. Any sudden movements or loud noises may startle the horse. At best it will run off; at worst it might trample you.

4. Move towards the horse gradually, talking to it in a low, soothing voice as you do so. Don't look into the horse's eyes, as it will see this as a threat.

5. When you are near the horse, stop and turn sideways.

6. This body language will be interpreted as 'come here' by the horse. Continue to approach the horse in this position until you are close enough to touch it.

7. Reach out your hand, making sure that your fingers are pressed together and not spread out. Gently stroke the horse's neck.

8. Continue to do this until the horse settles down, then gently but quickly slip a halter over its head.

HOW TO MAKE A FORTUNE FINDER

If your friends are wondering what might happen to them in the future, find out for them, using this fun fortune finder and your amazing skills of prediction!

You Will Need:
- a square piece of paper
- a pen.

What You Do

1. Fold the paper in half diagonally.

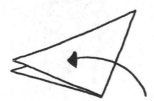

2. Do the same again to make a smaller triangle, then unfold, and lay it flat.

3. Fold each corner of the square into the centre, so the corners all meet at the middle.

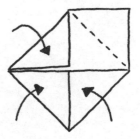

4. Turn the paper over and do the same again, folding each corner into the centre so that they meet in the middle.

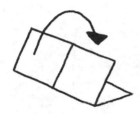

5. Turn the paper over so that you can see four squares. Fold the paper in half down the middle, with the squares on the outside.

6. Open the paper out so you can see the four squares again. Now fold the paper down the middle the other way.

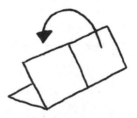

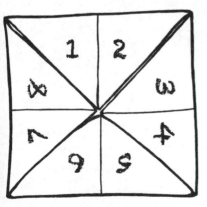

7. Write the name of four different colours on the four squares, then turn the fortune finder over. Write a different number on each of the eight triangles.

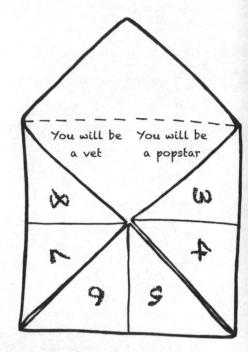

8. Lift up the triangles and write down a fortune for each number – how about 'You will become a billionaire'; 'You will live in Australia'; 'You will have six children'; 'You will fall in love when you are 19'; or 'You will become a famous surgeon'?

If you know which friends you'll be fortune-telling with, you could choose fortunes you know they'll love, and write them in the fortune finder.

Using Your Fortune Finder

1. Now you have your fortune finder – it's time to tell a friend's fortune. Slide your thumbs and forefingers under the four outside flaps and push the points of your fortune finder into the centre, so you can see the four colours.

2. Ask a friend to choose a colour. Spell out the name of the colour, while opening and closing the fortune finder for each letter.

3. When you come to the last letter, hold the fortune finder open and ask your friend to choose one of the numbers revealed. Count out that number, opening and closing the fortune finder as before.

4. Ask your friend to pick another number, and open the flap with that number on it. Then simply read your friend's fortune.

How To Be A Prima Ballerina

Becoming a prima ballerina takes hard work, dedication and regular lessons. To get you started, practise these basic positions.

Always keep your weight balanced evenly on both legs and make sure that your back is straight and that you are facing straight ahead.

First Position

Turn your feet out to the sides so that they form a straight line. Your heels should be touching. Make sure you are turning your whole leg out from the hip, not just your foot. Hold your hands out in front of you at waist height, so that they form an oval shape (imagine you are holding a beach ball in front of you).

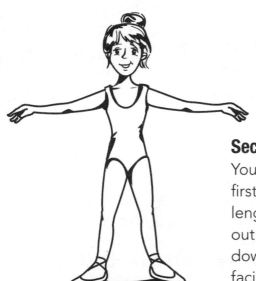

Second Position

Your feet should be placed as in first position, but spaced a foot's length apart. Stretch your arms out to the sides, angled slightly downwards, with your palms facing downward.

Third Position

With your toes still pointing out to the sides as in the first two positions, cross one foot halfway in front of the other, so that the heel is level with the arch of the foot behind.

One arm should be in first position (held out in front of you) and the other should be in second position (out to the side).

Fourth Position

This position is a little harder. With your toes still pointing out to the sides, bring one foot in front of the other with your toes and heels in line with each other. Make sure there is a space the length of one of your feet between the front and back foot.

One arm should be in second position and the other should be brought up in a curve above your head.

Fifth Position

This is the hardest position of them all. Place one foot exactly in front of the other, as in the fourth position, but they should be touching each other.

Bring both arms up in a curve so that they are above and slightly in front of your head.

How To Make
Spaghetti Jellyfish

Easy to make and seriously hilarious to serve, these spaghetti jellyfish will soon be your favourite supper treat.

You Will Need (For Two People):
- 2 jumbo frankfurters
- 24 strands of dried spaghetti.

What You Do
1. Cut each frankfurter into three equally sized pieces.

2. Break 24 strands of long spaghetti in half – so you have 48 shorter pieces of spaghetti. Push eight pieces of spaghetti into each piece of frankfurter – don't poke them all the way through.

3. Heat a saucepan of water until it is bubbling fiercely, then drop in your jellyfish and cook for seven minutes.

4. Remove each jellyfish with a slotted spoon and pop them on a plate. Enjoy them plain or with sauce.

How To Control The Weather

Who is going to believe you when you say that you are so powerful that you can control the weather? Well, show them who's in charge of the elements by creating your own rainbow or a flash of lightning.

Reveal A Rainbow

You Will Need:
- a sunny day
- a glass filled with water
- a sheet of white paper
- a table.

1. Place the glass so that it is half on and half off the edge of a table. Make sure the sun shines directly through the water on to the floor.

2. You will see a rainbow on the floor. Place the paper on the floor where the rainbow is, to see it clearly.

3. Ta da! You have a rainbow. It is formed by the light passing through the glass.

Electric Lightning

You Will Need:
- a woollen jumper or a piece of woollen cloth
- a balloon
- a paperclip.

1. This technique works best when the weather is very dry, so don't bother trying it on a misty, autumn day. Darken the room – the darker it is, the better you'll see your homemade lightning.

2. Put on the woollen jumper, or get your piece of woollen cloth ready.

3. Blow up the balloon and tie a knot in it.

4. Rub the balloon against your woollen jumper or piece of cloth about ten times, or for about 30 seconds.

5. Now hold the balloon close to the paperclip. You'll see a flash or spark, like lightning, jump between the balloon and the paperclip.

The lightning effect happens because you have created static electricity on the surface of the balloon which escapes by jumping towards the paperclip.

HOW TO LOOK YOUR BEST IN PHOTOS

Have you got photographs of yourself that you'd rather die than let anyone else see? Follow the simple tips below to look fabulous in every picture.

▸ Don't pose too much. The more natural you look, the better the photo.

▸ Stand straight with your head held high. Turn your body slightly to the side by putting one leg in front of the other, as shown below. This allows you to show your face and body in a 'semi-profile', which is very flattering.

▸ Smile – nobody looks good when they are miserable.

▸ You've probably been told to say 'Cheese', but this can make a smile look more like a grimace. For a natural, gentle smile that is easy to maintain, push your tongue against the back of your top teeth.

▸ Open your eyes wide (not too wide or you'll look startled or slightly crazy).

▸ Don't stare directly at the camera, as this may result in your eyes looking red in the photograph. Direct your gaze at a spot just slightly above the camera.

▸ Relax as much as you can. Just before the photograph is taken, take a deep breath and then breathe out.

HOW TO READ SOMEONE'S PALM

The art of reading someone's palm to predict their future and reveal their personality is called palmistry. Master it and you're guaranteed to be the centre of attention at any party.

This diagram shows you the main lines you might find on a person's palm. Not everyone has every line, and some may be better defined or longer in some people than in others. Take a good look at your friend's right hand and then use the following clues to reveal their future.

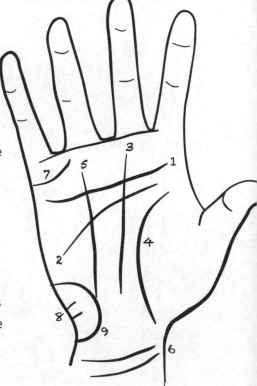

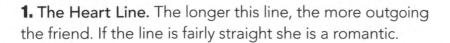

1. The Heart Line. The longer this line, the more outgoing the friend. If the line is fairly straight she is a romantic.

2. The Head Line. This line offers clues about your friend's personality. If it is curved she is spontaneous, but if it is straight she is practical and won't let her heart rule her head. The deeper the line, the more imaginative the person.

3. The Fate Line. Not everybody has this line, but those who do tend to be responsible and purposeful.

4. The Life Line. A long life line means that your friend is vivacious and relishes life. A shorter line means her health is good. If the line is faint, she is indecisive.

5. The Sun Line. A short sun line indicates future success and a long one predicts wealth and happiness. If the line ends in a kind of star shape, your friend is destined to be famous.

6. The Luck Line. An unbroken luck line means 30 years of good fortune. Gaps in the line point to less fortunate periods in life.

7. The Relationship Line. A long, horizontal relationship line means your friend will have one important, happy relationship. More than one line predicts that she will

have several relationships during her lifetime. If the line curves upward her relationships will be successful. A downward curve points to a messy breakup.

8. Travel Lines. The more of these lines your friend has, the more she loves to travel.

9. The Intuition Line. People who have this are usually insightful.

How To Confuse Your Brain And Body

Prepare to be amazed! There are many ways to confuse your brain and your body. Here are two very simple – but hugely effective – methods to try. Why not have a go with a friend?

Say When
Ask your friend to hold her bare left arm out straight with the inside of her elbow facing upwards. Tell her that you are going to stroke your finger up the skin of her arm and she must shout when your finger reaches the dip at the inside of her elbow.

Ask her to close her eyes and concentrate. Start stroking the inside of her arm above her wrist. Gradually work your way up to the dip until she says stop. Chances are she'll find it hard to be accurate.

Mix Up

Ask your friend to stretch out her arms, and cross one over the other so her palms are pressed together.

Tell her to interlace her fingers, then bring her hands down and under, towards her, so she can hold them next to her chest.

Ask her to move the middle finger of her right hand. You can point to the finger, but don't touch it. She will probably find it hard to do, as her brain is confused by the strange position of her fingers.

HOW TO SURVIVE IN THE DESERT

The most important thing to do when you find yourself alone in the desert is to find shelter from the sun. Look for shadows cast by scrub vegetation or rocks. Shelter during the day and travel by night, when it is much cooler.

Construct A Solar Still

The biggest problem you will face is the lack of water. To ensure you have a source of water, construct a 'solar still'.

You Will Need:
- a plastic bag
- scissors
- something to dig with
- a cup
- some stones.

1. Take a plastic bag and cut down one side seam and along the bottom edge. Open it out so you have a large plastic sheet.

2. Dig a shallow hole.

3. In the middle of the hole place a cup upright in the sand, below the level of the ground.

4. Cover the hole with the plastic sheet and anchor it with stones around its edge. Place a small stone in the middle of the plastic so it is directly above the cup.

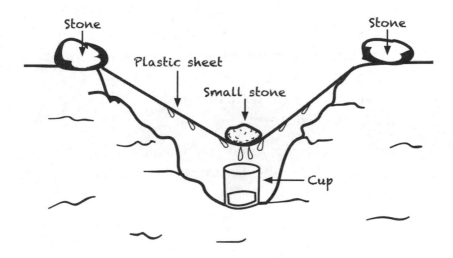

5. Water vapour will condense underneath the plastic sheet and drip into the cup.

Essential Survival Tips

▸ Your solar still will not provide much water, so you need to conserve as much of your bodily fluids as possible. The biggest cause of water loss is sweating. Don't cry, talk or pant in the heat – you need to keep your mouth closed and breathe through your nose. This reduces the amount of water you lose from your body. Make sure your movements are slow and regular to keep your sweating to a minimum.

▸ When you are hot you will want to take off your clothes. Don't. Keep as much of your body covered as possible to protect your skin from the sun and hot winds. If you have a hat keep it on to protect you from sunstroke and to conserve moisture. If you don't have a hat tie a piece of cloth around your head. Make sure it hangs over the back of your neck.

▸ Watch out for signs that you are suffering from too much heat. You will start to feel very tired and disorientated.

▸ Check the colour of your wee. If it is a dark browny yellow, you are dehydrated. The moment you are aware of any of these warning signs drink a few sips of water. Continue to drink a little water every hour.

▸ The large expanse of mostly empty terrain in deserts will cause you to underestimate distances. As a general rule, things are about three times further away than you think.

▸ Sandstorms are frequent in the desert. If you get caught in one, stay calm. Look for something to shelter behind. Cover your nose and mouth with clothing and lie down flat, with your back to the wind, until it has passed.

HOW TO ANNOY PEOPLE IN A LIFT

A lift is the perfect place to practise your stand-up comedy routine – think about it, you've got a captive audience who can't go anywhere until the lift stops. Turn the page for some hilarious ideas.

▶ Grin at another passenger and then announce, 'I've got new socks on.'

▶ Crash from side to side as if you're sailing in rough seas.

▶ Suggest you all join in a singalong.

▶ Say 'Ding!' at each floor.

▶ Salute and say 'Welcome aboard,' every time someone gets into the lift.

▶ Open your bag and, while peering inside, ask, 'Got enough air in there?'

▶ Meow occasionally.

▶ Stand silent and motionless in the corner, facing the wall, without getting off when the lift stops.

▶ Make racing-car noises when anyone comes into the lift.

▶ Ask everyone for a high-five when the lift stops.

▶ Spin around and around in the centre of the lift.

Don't get so carried away that you forget to get off at the right floor.

How To Work Out Your Dog's 'Human Age'

Adog can be a girl's best friend, but your canine pal grows up a bit faster than you. Here are some ways of calculating the age of a dog in human terms.

A well-known method says that one dog year is equal to seven human years. Except that at one, a dog is more like a teenager, and almost fully grown – unlike a seven-year-old human.

A more accurate method, for breeds of dog that have an average lifespan of about 12 years, is to start with the age of 15 for the dog's first year, add ten years for its second, and then add five for each year of the dog's life after that.

Age Of Dog	'Human Age'
1	15
2	25
3	30
4	35
5	40
6	45
7	50

How To Make
A Friendship Bracelet

These make great gifts to swap with your friends.
Start by practising with four or five strands of
thread. Once you've got the hang of it, you can use
as many different threads as you like to make really
colourful, chunky bracelets.

1. Choose four strands of yarn or embroidery
thread in different colours, each about
60 centimetres long. Bind them together
with a knot at the top. Tape the knotted end
to something to secure the bracelet while
you work – try the back of a chair.

2. Take the first thread on the left (thread **A**) and wrap it over and around thread **B** to make a knot, as shown above. Hold thread **B** so that it is taut when you do this and make sure the knot is tight. Repeat this to make a double knot.

3. Still using thread **A**, make a double knot around thread **C**, and then finally around **D**. When you have completed the first row, thread **A** will be on the right and thread **B** (the next thread you will be working with) will be on the left.

4. Repeat steps **2** and **3** with thread **B**, then **C**, and then **D**. Then start with **A** again. When your bracelet is long enough to go around your wrist, tie the ends together in another firm knot.

5. To wear it, tie the two knotted ends together around your wrist.

HOW TO SURVIVE A SHOAL OF PIRANHAS

You might have heard that a shoal of vicious piranha fish can strip a human being to her skeleton in a matter of seconds, but this is just not true.

In reality, these toothy fish don't live up to their fearsome reputation. Some are actually even vegetarians. Even the most dangerous piranhas do not prey on large mammals (like you). It is true, however, that a piranha fish can give you a very nasty nip – in fact it could easily bite off a toe.

Here are some tips on how to hang on to all your digits in piranha-infested waters.

Preventive Measures

▸ Be aware of piranha habitats – they live in slow-moving rivers, streams and lakes in South America. The most dangerous type is the red-bellied piranha.

▸ Don't enter any of the large pools that can form beside rivers after heavy rainfall. Piranhas might have become trapped in these pools and, if they have, they will be very hungry indeed, and much more likely to attack.

▸ The dry season can also be a dangerous time to go into the rivers of South America – piranha prey can be in short supply during this time, so they will be peckish.

▸ Avoid water close to rubbish dumps, or trees where birds nest – these can be rich sources of food for piranhas, so the fish are more likely to lurk there.

▸ Piranha fish can sense blood in the water, so don't enter the water if you have a bleeding cut anywhere on your body.

▸ If you do see piranhas, don't panic – thrashing about will only attract them and other predators. Move calmly and smoothly through the water to the bank, where you can get out and panic in relative safety.

HOW TO MAKE A PIÑATA

Make your next party a Mexican-style fiesta, with a fabulous piñata. A piñata is a decoration filled with sweets or small gifts. The best part is that a piñata has to be bashed open with a stick to get at the goodies.

You Will Need:
- a balloon
- a piece of thick string at least 60cm long
- newspaper
- paintbrush
- a mixture of 250ml water and 250ml PVA glue
- a pin
- scissors
- sticky tape
- 5 sheets of A4 card
- paperclips
- poster paint
- a blindfold
- a stick
- tissue paper.

What You Do
1. Blow up your balloon and tie a knot in the neck. Rest the balloon in a small bowl to stop it wobbling about.

2. Tear the newspaper into strips, dip them in the PVA glue and water mixture and use them to cover the balloon completely. Wait until it's completely dry, then add another layer. Repeat until you have added five layers of newspaper.

3. Once the final layer is dry, cover the whole thing with the diluted glue and leave it overnight to dry thoroughly.

4. Pop the balloon inside using a pin. Cut a flap in the paper shell and remove the balloon. Check the inside of your piñata is dry, then fill it with sweets. Reseal the flap with sticky tape.

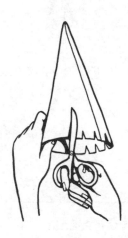

5. Use a sheet of card to make a cone shape and stick it together with glue (secure it with paperclips while the glue dries). Cut off the triangular ends at the base of your cone. Repeat with the other four sheets of card.

6. Take each cone and make small cuts, about 1 centimetre deep, around the base.

7. Put glue on the underside of the flaps and use them to stick the cones to the piñata, making a star shape. You'll need to hold them in place to make sure they stick properly.

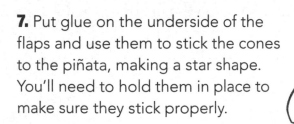

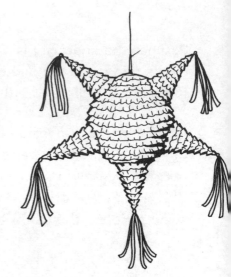

8. Once your star piñata is dry, paint it with brightly coloured poster paints.

Smashing

Use the end of your scissors to pierce a hole in the top of your piñata. Attach the length of string and hang it from a tree branch or a washing line. Everyone takes a turn to be blindfolded and bash the piñata with a stick until it breaks.

> For a truly Mexican look, decorate your piñata with strips of tissue paper with cuts 1cm deep in them, to make a frill. Glue the uncut edges to the piñata, overlapping the strips each time.

HOW TO MAKE SENSE WHILE TALKING NONSENSE

When two words or phrases that seem to contradict each other are put together, the figure of speech they make is called an 'oxymoron'. Oxymorons don't make any sense, but they also make complete sense and are ideal for baffling your friends. Here are some to use:

▸ Pretty ugly

▸ Deafening silence

▸ Constant change

▸ Least favourite

▸ Exact estimate

▸ Small crowd

▸ Instant classic

▸ Liquid gas

▸ Advanced beginner

▸ Open secret

▸ Alone together

HOW TO SET A WORLD RECORD

If you think you're the fastest, the slowest, the best, or maybe even the worst in the world, here's how to register a world record officially.

First you need to decide whether you want to set a new record or break an existing one. If you choose a completely new record, you will need to contact 'Guinness World Records', the organization that judges, records and publishes a famous book containing many world records every year. You can go to their website for all the details of registering a record-breaking attempt. You will find it at www.guinnessworldrecords.com.

Tell Guinness exactly what record attempt you are planning. They'll let you know if they think it's a suitable idea. If they do, they will detail exactly what evidence you need to provide to show you set the record fairly and squarely. If they think your idea is too dangerous or too difficult to prove, they won't accept it.

You may choose to break an existing record – and there are all sorts from which to choose – rolling an orange with your nose, egg-throwing and marathon kissing are all possibilities. Guinness will tell you the details of the current record, the guidelines you need to follow, and the evidence you need to provide. In some cases, they will send a someone to witness your record attempt.

Once you've submitted details of your record attempt, Guinness will let you know within a few weeks whether or not you've proved your claim. If you have, you are a record breaker!

HOW TO MAKE BUBBLE BATH

Here's a quick and simple way to make some luxurious bubble bath that you can enjoy when treating yourself to a well-deserved pampering session. Alternatively, put some in a pretty glass bottle and give it to your best friend as a present.

1. In a clean bowl, mix together two cups of clear or light-coloured shampoo, three cups of water and two teaspoons of salt. Stir the mixture gently until it thickens slightly.

2. Pour a tiny amount of red food colouring into your mixture and stir again. Keep adding the food colouring until the mixture is a perfect pink colour.

3. Add ten drops of an essential oil for a wonderful scent. Rose, lavender, ylang-ylang, sandalwood, marjoram, myrrh, rosewood and camomile have relaxing and luxurious scents.

4. Pour the bubble bath into a bottle and seal.

HOW TO BECOME A FAMOUS ACTRESS

D o you dream of fans adoring you, of travelling by private jet, and seeing giant posters of yourself all over the place? Follow the tips below and a life of superstardom may be yours:

▸ Pay extra attention in drama lessons. Take an acting course outside school as well, if possible.

▸ Practise as much as you can and take part in school productions and local theatre groups – you need talent, but experience helps.

▸ To start off your career, try to get work as an 'extra' – these are people with non-speaking roles who appear in the background of movies and TV dramas. Be prepared to take whatever roles are offered.

▸ Never turn down a party invitation: you never know who you might meet – a talent-spotter or a famous director.

▸ Get a professional photograph taken of your head and shoulders (known in the business as a 'headshot'). List all your acting experience on the back. If you have other talents and abilities, such as singing, parachuting, ice-skating, martial arts or Irish dancing, list them, too – they might be just what a director is looking for. Don't list anything you really can't do in case you are asked to prove it.

▸ You'll need an agent to help you land big roles and handle all the financial and legal negotiations that go on in the film business. Send copies of your headshots to as many agents as possible.

▸ Move to a big city. If you've set your heart on being a star in Hollywood, this will have to be Los Angeles.

▸ Practise looking glamorous, and get a friend to pretend to be your assistant – she should constantly shout into a mobile phone and carry lots of papers that look like film scripts.

▸ Contacts are vital. Maintain good relationships with directors, agents and fellow actors by being polite, punctual and professional at all times.

▸ Develop a thick skin. When you're in the limelight you'll receive lots of flattery and lots of criticism. Try to ignore both, unless they come from someone whose opinion you trust.

How To Create An Optical Illusion

This origami project is based on an optical illusion that tricks the brain into thinking that it is seeing one complete picture rather than two different pictures in quick succession. Find a piece of card about 5cm by 5cm and follow the steps below.

1. Fold corner **A** backwards and corner **B** forwards, along the dotted lines.

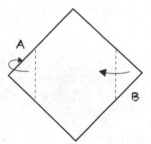

2. Draw a a small picture on one side of the piece of card.

3. Draw a different shape on the other side. Make this picture larger than the first picture, but make sure you don't draw on the folded corners.

Blow here

4. Hold the card between your thumb and forefinger, as shown. Blow hard on to one of the folded edges.

5. The card will spin and you will see the two pictures as one.

Another famous optical illusion like this is the bird in the cage. Draw a bird on one side of the card, and a birdcage on the other, then follow the instructions and hey presto – the bird is in the cage.

HOW TO AVOID
A SHARK ATTACK

You are very, very unlikely to be attacked by a shark. But it's a good idea to reduce the risk as much as you can. Being eaten alive ruins any trip to the seaside.

▸ You could eliminate the risk of a shark attack completely by not swimming in the sea at all. Failing that, you could stay out of the sea in shark-attack hotspots, such as the eastern United States (especially Florida), which has more shark attacks than any other part of the world.

▸ Listen out for warnings on the radio or TV of shark sightings in the area you are staying.

▶ Don't swim in the sea on your own. Sharks are more likely to attack lone swimmers than a group.

▶ Your swimsuit could attract a shark if it's brightly coloured or has strong, contrasting colours – sharks can't see very well, so they're likely to take an interest in anything that stands out. Don't wear jewellery or anything shiny, as a shark could mistake it for fish scales flashing in the water.

▶ Avoid lots of splashing about, which can interest a shark because it could be a creature in distress.

▶ Don't go swimming at dawn and dusk, or at night – sharks are likely to feed at those times.

▶ Sharks often lurk near sandbars and steep drop-offs: stay away from them, or look out for a fin slicing through the water towards you.

▶ Sharks are well known for their ability to detect blood in the water from kilometres away. Don't go swimming in the sea if you have an open cut anywhere on your body.

▶ Sharks feed on smaller fish and marine mammals. Don't go swimming in areas where there are likely to be lots of these 'bait' creatures – you could find yourself in the middle of a shark snack bar. Diving sea birds are a sign that there are plenty of bait fish in the sea. If you see people fishing it is a sure sign that bait creatures are around.

How To Eat With Chopsticks

Next time you eat Chinese food, why not ditch the knife and fork and try eating the traditional way, with chopsticks? It's easier than you think.

> Most people try to move both chopsticks, and their food ends up slipping out from between the sticks. The trick is to keep one chopstick still, and move the other one to meet it.

1. To set up the bottom chopstick, place it between your thumb and middle finger. It should rest on the space between your thumb and index finger, as shown in the diagram here. Keep your index finger out of the way.

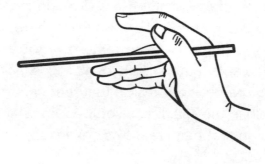

2. For the top chopstick, hold the second chopstick between your thumb and index finger, with the side of it resting against the tip of your thumb and the tip of your index finger resting on top of the chopstick.

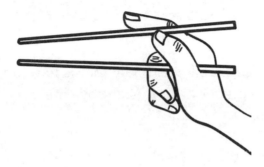

3. The bottom chopstick should always remain still. Practise moving the top chopstick towards the bottom one. Once you have got the hang of this, try picking objects up with your chopsticks until you are ready to progress to food.

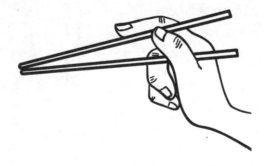

HOW TO REMEMBER THE PLANETS IN THE SOLAR SYSTEM

Your lessons are full of tricky things to remember, but here's a great way to make those memory missions a little easier.

Starting with the planet closest to the Sun, the eight planets in the solar system are:

Mercury Venus Earth Mars
Jupiter Saturn Uranus
Neptune

To help you memorize the planets in the correct order, use one of these strange sentences:

My Very Educated Mother
Just Served Up Newts

or

My Vole Eats Mother's Jam
Sandwiches Uncommonly
Nicely.

The first letter of each word matches the first letter of each planet. This method of remembering information is called a 'mnemonic'. Why not make up your own mnemonics, about anything you find tricky to remember?

HOW TO KEEP A MESSAGE SECRET

If you master the art of making your own invisible ink and learn how to make it visible again, you can write secret messages to your friends. Anyone who's not in on the secret will just see a blank piece of paper.

You Will Need:
- tap water
- baking soda
- a bowl
- a toothpick or cotton bud
- a sheet of paper
- a light, such as a desk lamp.

1. First mix equal amounts of water and baking soda in a bowl. A little goes a long way, so you won't need very much of either ingredient.

2. Dip a toothpick or cotton bud into the mixture and write your message on a sheet of paper.

3. To reveal the message simply hold the paper up to a lightbulb (don't make contact with it or you will singe the paper). You'll see the message appear in brown as the heat produced by the bulb reacts with the baking soda.

You are now ready to communicate in complete secrecy.

Another way of revealing the message is to brush some purple grape juice over the paper using a paintbrush. The baking soda and grape juice react together and change the colour of the writing.

How To Make A Compass

Here's a method of making a simple compass for when you get caught short without this vital piece of kit.

1. Pick a flat leaf and allow it to float on the surface of a cup that is full of water.

2. Find a sewing needle. Holding the eye of the needle, wipe the point down the side of a magnet.

3. When you get to the bottom of the magnet, lift the needle off and away. Then move the point back to the top of the magnet before you stroke again. This ensures that you stroke the magnet in one direction only.

4. Repeat at least 50 times. This has the effect of magnetizing the needle.

5. If you don't have a magnet you could use a silk cloth to magnetize the needle, but the effects will be much weaker.

6. Carefully lay the needle on the top of the leaf, and watch as the leaf slowly turns. The needle will eventually line up along the line of the Earth's north and south magnetic poles, with its tip pointing north.

How To Avoid Being Chomped By A Hippo

If you think hippos are chilled-out mud-wallowers, think again – they can be very aggressive. They tend to attack if they think someone is trespassing on their territory. They are huge animals, with razor-sharp, tusk-like teeth. Hippos have even been known to bite crocodiles in half.

You might want to stay away from hippo habitats, but here are a few tips just in case:

Emergency Tactics

▸ Keep as far away from the hippo as you can. There are two types of hippo to avoid particularly – female hippos protecting their young and hungry hippos short of food during a drought.

▸ If a hippo opens its jaws, it isn't yawning – far from being bored, it is showing you that it has very big teeth and could attack at any moment.

▸ Show that you're not a threat by backing away slowly. If the hippo sees that you're moving out of its territory, it might not feel the need to help you on your way by taking a large bite out of you.

▸ Try and make sure you're downwind of the hippo, so that the wind isn't carrying your scent straight up the hippo's nostrils, and sending angry messages to its brain.

▸ Never block a hippo's path to water. This is guaranteed to make it cross.

▸ Running away won't help, because a hippo will easily outrun you. As a last resort, run as fast as you can to the nearest tree – climb it and shout for help.

HOW TO MAKE A FROG TAKE THE LONG JUMP

Follow this origami project and you will end up with a frog that, with practice, can be made to leap two metres long or about 60 centimetres high. Why not have a jumping competition with friends?

1. Cut a rectangle 8cm by 5cm from the cardboard of an old cereal packet.

2. Fold and unfold corner **A** diagonally to **D**, and then **B** diagonally to **C**, forming a cross which takes up two thirds of the rectangle.

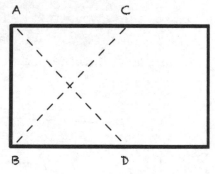

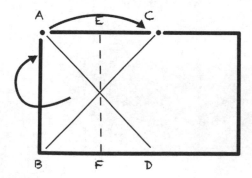

3. Next, fold and unfold the card along the line marked **E** and **F** as shown.

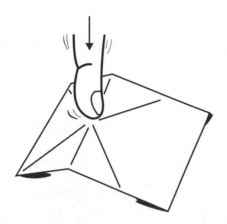

4. Push down the centre point where the three folds meet. The card should pop inside out.

5. Refold all the creases, push points **E** and **F** inwards, and then fold the top (**A/B**) across to points **C** and **D**.

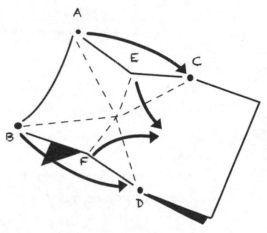

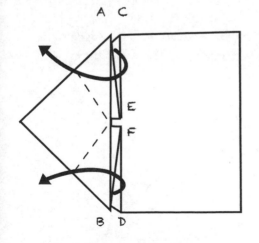

6. Your card should end up looking like this. Fold up corners **A** and **B**, as shown here.

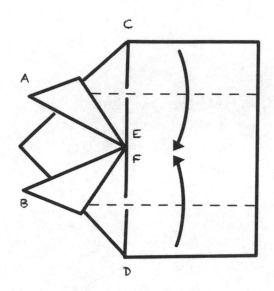

7. Fold in points **C** and **D** as shown here.

8. Make a Z-shaped pleat (this means a gentle crease, not a hard fold) by creasing half way along the frog's body and then again, a quarter of the way along its body.

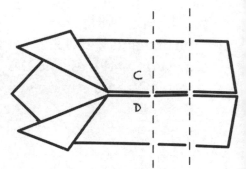

9. To make your frog jump, press down on its back edge, then slide your finger off really quickly, so the frog flicks up into the air.

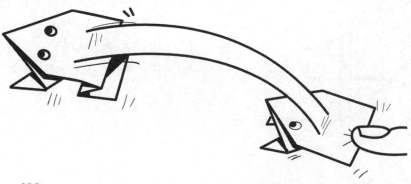

How To Write 'Happy Birthday' In Ten Different Languages

With this helpful guide, you'll be a huge hit at any international birthday celebration.

Around The World

- ▶ Bengali ...   Shubho Jonmodin

- ▶ Danish ...   Tillykke med fødselsdagen

- ▶ Dutch ...   Gelukkige verjaardag

- ▶ Finnish ...   Hyvää syntymäpäivää!

- ▶ French ...   Joyeux anniversaire

- ▶ German ...   Alles Gute zum Geburtstag

- ▶ Hawaiian ...   Hau'oli La Hanau

- ▶ Portuguese ...   Parabens Feliz aniversario

- ▶ Italian ...   Buon compleanno

- ▶ Spanish ...   Feliz cumpleaños

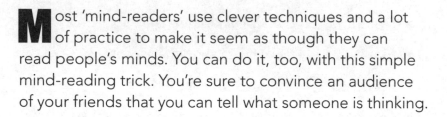

How To Read Someone's Mind

Most 'mind-readers' use clever techniques and a lot of practice to make it seem as though they can read people's minds. You can do it, too, with this simple mind-reading trick. You're sure to convince an audience of your friends that you can tell what someone is thinking.

You Will Need:
- a magician's hat (or a bowl with high sides)
- paper cut into strips
- a pen
- an A4 pad.

What You Do
1. Ask your friends to call out the names of ten celebrities. As the first one is called out, write it down on a slip of paper, fold it up and put it into the hat.

2. When the second name is called out, pretend to write it down on another slip of paper but, instead, write down the first name again. Fold it and put it into the hat.

3. Do the same thing for all the other names – until you have ten slips of paper in the hat, all with the same name on them.

4. Ask one friend to choose a slip of paper from the hat. Tell her that she is not to read it out loud nor let you see it, but to concentrate on the name.

5. Look at her intently and place your hands on either side of your head, as though a mysterious force is at work.

6. After a few moments nod, then write the first famous name on an A4 pad, large enough for your whole audience to read.

7. Ask your friend to reveal the name of the person she picked out of the hat to the audience, as you turn over the A4 pad. They will be amazed.

Warning. Remove the magician's hat quickly before anyone investigates the other slips of paper inside it.

How To Deal With Bullies

Most people have been bullied at some time in their lives. If you're being bullied it's not your fault – the bully is the one with the problem, but you must take some action.

▸ Find a teacher, parent or adult you trust, and tell them what is happening. They don't have to get involved or even speak to the bully. Just sharing the problem will make you feel better, and they can support, advise, and help you stand up for yourself. Schools have strict policies on bullying and your teachers will have lots of experience of dealing with the problem.

▸ Practise looking and sounding confident. Bullies are usually cowards who pick on people that they think are weaker than themselves. Stand up tall and hold your head up high when you walk around the school. Speak in a clear, strong voice and look people straight in the eye.

▸ Whenever possible, ignore any behaviour that is intended to make you feel scared or bad about yourself. Convince the bully that you are not bothered by them or hurt by their words – they'll quickly get bored and leave you alone.

▸ Try to think of ways to deal with difficult situations before they occur. Practise things that you could say to someone taunting you. Crying or shouting usually only makes things worse, whereas a clever, casual remark, which is neither rude nor sarcastic, will make you seem confident and in control. Always try to remain calm and be reasonable.

▸ Bullies won't pick on someone who is surrounded by supportive friends. Keep an eye out for the people who often seem to be alone and make an effort to get to know them. This way you'll make lots of new friends and keep the bullies at bay.

> No one deserves to be bullied. Don't give in to a bully, don't encourage a bully, and never, ever be a bully yourself.

HOW TO SKIM STONES

Making a stone bounce across the surface of a lake or river takes skill. With a bit of practice you might even be able to beat the current world record of 51 bounces …

1. Choose a flat, oval-shaped stone that fits easily inside your palm and find an area of calm water, such as a lake or pond. Stand side-on to the water and crouch with your feet apart.

2. Curl your index finger around the edge of the stone and place your thumb flat on top of it. Your middle finger should be underneath, making sure the stone stays horizontal when you throw it.

3. Draw back your arm and then jerk it forward, using your wrist and index finger to spin the stone as it leaves your hand.

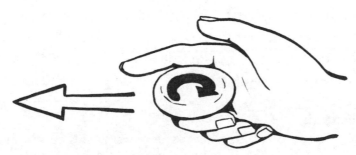

You need to throw the stone as near to the surface of the water as you can, and almost parallel to it. If you want to be technical, you're aiming for an angle of around 20° between the path of the stone and the surface of the water.

The front of the stone should be a little higher than the back to give it a better chance of bouncing.

How To Make A Pom-Pom

Pom-poms are incredibly easy to make and you can use them to decorate many things. Customize your clothes by sewing them on to scarves and woolly hats, or even hang them on the Christmas tree. Wool comes in a huge variety of colours and textures, so get creative …

You Will Need:
- wool
- a pen
- a pair of scissors
- a piece of stiff cardboard to make the pom-pom template.

1. Draw two identical circles on the cardboard (try tracing around a circular object, such as a tin). The bigger the circles, the larger your pom-pom will be.

2. Draw a smaller circle inside each of the large circles.

Cut out the large circles, and then cut out the inner circles, so that you have two ring-shaped pieces of card.

3. Take the wool you want to use and cut it into 1-metre lengths.

4. Lay the two rings on top of one another, trapping one end of the wool between the two pieces of card. Feed the other end of the wool across the ring and through the hole.

5. When you have used up the wool, start wrapping a new piece. You don't need to tie it to the last one – just make sure that the end of it is lined up with the outer edge of the rings.

6. Keep wrapping until the hole is so tiny you can't get the wool through.

7. Slip the blades of your scissors through the wool and between the two pieces of card. Cut the wool all around the outside edge of the rings.

8. Take another length of wool and slip it between the two rings. Tie it in a firm knot around the wool which passes through the hole in the rings. Slip the cardboard rings off and fluff up your pom-pom.

HOW TO EXPLAIN WHY YOU ARE LATE FOR SCHOOL

It's always a good idea to have a few excuses up your sleeve should you ever be late for school (through no fault of your own, of course).

▸ I came all the way to school before I realized I still had my pyjamas on, and had to go home and change.

▸ When I got here my teacher wasn't in the classroom, so I went out looking for her.

▸ I was abducted by aliens for experimental purposes. I have been gone for fifty years, but fortunately in Earth time it was only an hour.

▸ I invented a time machine that took me forward to my exam results. I saw that I get straight As, so I thought I might as well take things easy from now on.

▸ I was helping Little Bo Peep find her sheep.

▸ I squeezed the toothpaste too hard, and spent all morning getting it back in the tube.

▸ My parents lost the keys to my cage.

▸ I'm afraid I can't tell you why I'm late. The Government has sworn me to secrecy.

▸ I'm not late … everyone else is early.

▸ I had a dream and I was top of the class, so I didn't bother getting out of bed.

How To Survive On A Desert Island

Have you ever thought about what you'd do if you were marooned on a desert island? Here's how to make the best of the situation until help arrives …

Thirsty Work

Nobody can survive for more than a few days without drinking water. In the heat of a desert island, you will be sweating a lot and dehydrating rapidly. Finding water is your first priority.

With luck there will be fresh water flowing on your island. Search along the shore for a stream running into the sea. Follow the stream back towards its source as far as you can. When you can go no further, check that the water is running clear and that it doesn't smell bad before you drink any. Only drink a tiny amount at first and increase day by day. This allows you to check it is safe to drink before you have consumed too much.

If you can't find a source of fresh water, you will need to collect water. There are two main methods. First, make sure you have any containers available positioned to collect rainwater when it falls. Store the water somewhere cold and shady during the day to stop

it evaporating. Second, every morning you should collect the dew that has formed on the leaves of plants – this is perfect for drinking. Mop it up with a clean cloth and wring the cloth into a container.

Take Shelter

It is essential to stay out of the heat of the sun on your island, so the next thing to do is make a shelter. Look for something that could form the basis of your shelter, such as a dry rocky outcrop, a fallen tree, or even a cave. Gather reeds, twigs, and large leaves and use them to finish your shelter. You could try weaving branches together. Line the shelter with dry leaves, pine needles or bracken.

Food

Some doctors say a human being can survive without food for four to six weeks. However, if you leave it for more than a few days you will be too weak to look for food when you need it. Why not make a fishing rod with string, a stick and a safety pin as a hook, and see if you have any luck landing a fish? Alternatively you could attempt to spear fish with a sharpened stick. Failing that, most seaweed is edible, though you might have to boil it for a while.

Coconuts are a great source of food and drink, and hopefully these will be falling from the trees on your island. The skill is to open them.

1. Once you have removed the green outer layer, pull off the 'husk' – the hairy outer layer.

2. At one end of the coconut, you'll see three dents – like two eyes and a mouth. Hold that end in one hand. Find the 'seam' that runs between the eyes. Follow the seam to the middle of the coconut. Imagine a line running around its fattest part.

3. Find a large rock and give the coconut some hard taps along this line. Keep turning the coconut so you hit it all the way round the seam. After a few good whacks, the coconut should break into two halves.

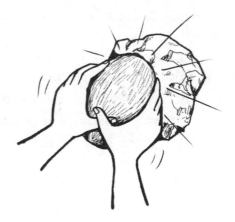

4. Scrape out the white 'meat' inside with a sharp shell or piece of rock. Smell the inside of the coconut before you eat it. If it smells sour or mouldy, throw it away.

How To Build A House Of Cards

Are you looking for something to while away a rainy afternoon? Do you have lots of patience and a steady hand? Why not build a house of cards? All you need is a deck of playing cards and a draught-free bedroom.

Master Builder
1. Find a flat surface that isn't too slippery – a short-pile carpet is ideal. Grab an old pack of cards – brand new cards, which are shiny and slippery, are far more difficult to use for a house of cards than old ones.

2. Lean two cards against one another – shortest ends at the top and bottom – to make an upside-down 'V', that looks like a tent. They should be about the same width apart at the bottom as your middle three fingers. This forms the basis of the whole house of cards.

3. Place another tent shape right beside the first one.

4. Place a playing card horizontally across the top of the two tent shapes, to form the floor of your house's second storey.

5. To complete a very small house put another tent shape on top. However, girls who like to be the best at everything probably want to make a bigger, far more impressive house of cards. To do this, you'll need to add three more storeys to create the classic house of cards shown here.

You will need plenty of patience. Don't expect to be a master builder the first time you try.

Warning. No self-respecting builder of card houses would cheat. The cards should stand up because of your amazing balancing skills and not because they've been stuck together with sticky tape!

How To Win

Stand facing a friend and stare into each other's eyes. The first person to blink or look away loses the contest. It's not as easy as it sounds. Your eyes dry out if you don't blink, and they start to sting. Follow these tips to be unbeatable.

▸ Before the contest starts, close your eyes as tightly as you can, and for as long as you can, to produce tears that will keep your eyes moist.

▸ Use eye drops before the contest. (Technically, this is cheating, so make sure nobody spots you doing it.)

A STARING CONTEST

▸ Open your eyes wide during the contest and, when you think you are about to blink, open them even wider. This goes against your natural instincts, but will actually make your eyes water, thus keeping them moist.

▸ When you are about to blink, squint and furrow your brow. Again, this will produce tears and help you to keep staring for longer.

> Never have a staring contest with a goldfish – they never blink!

How To Bling Up Your Bag

Use your design skills to give a boring bag some super style.

Heart Felt
You'll love these gorgeous hearts …

You Will Need:
- a pencil
- several sheets of white paper
- sheets of coloured craft foam or felt
- scissors
- PVA glue
- fake jewels
- self-adhesive hook-and-loop tape.

What You Do

1. Draw a selection of heart shapes in different sizes on a sheet of paper – you can trace over the ones shown here. Cut them out.

2. Draw around your paper templates on the foam or felt. Use several contrasting colours. Cut out the shapes.

3. Dab some glue in the middle of the largest heart and stick the next largest heart on to it. Keep going until you've used them all. Why not add a fake jewel on the final layer?

4. Fix a square of hook-and-loop tape to your bag, and another to the back of your heart – then press the bag and the heart together.

Try using different designs: stars, flowers or animal shapes, for example.

How To Make A Kite

Kite flying is the perfect activity for a windy day. Just grab a friend, and find an open spot that's not too crowded. Oh, and you'll need a kite, too, and that's where these instructions will come in handy.

You Will Need:
- a tabloid-size newspaper
- sticky tape
- a ruler
- a pencil
- scissors
- 23m of string
- coloured paper or ribbons.

1. Make the body of the kite using two double pages from the middle of a tabloid-size newspaper. Join the bottom of one double sheet to the top of the other with sticky tape to make a large rectangle.

2. To shape your kite, use a ruler to measure 18 centimetres in from each of the four corners, and mark the correct distances with a pencil. Join up the marks as shown in the drawing below. Use a pair of scissors to cut along the lines.

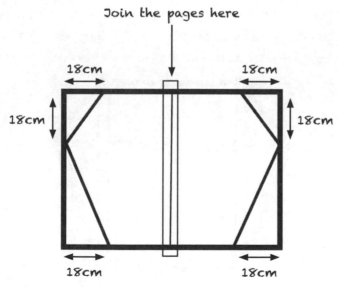

3. You need to strengthen your kite with sticky tape. Tape all along the edges of the kite and across it horizontally and vertically, as shown in this drawing.

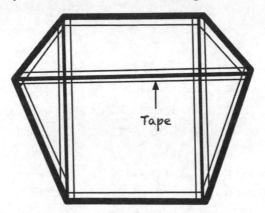

4. Take two more double pages of the newspaper and make two tight tubes – start at one corner and roll them up across diagonally until you reach the other corner. Tape the tubes on to the kite as shown here.

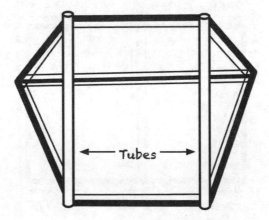

5. Take 1.5 metres of string and tape one end to the left-hand top corner of the kite, and the other end to the right-hand corner. Tie a piece of string 20 metres long to the middle of this string to make your fly line.

6. Take another piece of string 1.5 metres long and tape it across the two bottom edges of your kite. The tail is attached to this string. You can make a tail from coloured paper or ribbons.

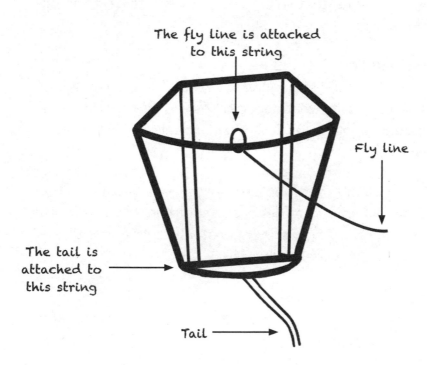

The fly line is attached to this string

Fly line

The tail is attached to this string

Tail →

HOW TO BE FRIENDS WITH A VAMPIRE

You may have read a vampire book, or seen a film or TV show about them, but how easy would it really be to have a vampire for a friend? If you don't mind their eating habits, try these helpful pointers to be a vampire's perfect pal.

Blending In

To make your vampire friend feel at ease and to help them blend in, wear dark clothes yourself. Blood red is a great colour for accessories, and a floor-length cape is a fashion-must.

Why not knit your friend some gloves, a hat and a chunky scarf? Vampires are dead, and therefore have no blood circulation, so their skin is constantly cold to the touch and they may feel chills easily.

Out And About

Don't suggest meeting up at midday. All your meetings with your new 'BFF' will have to take place under cover of darkness, as they can't stand the sun.

Never take your vampire friend to the hairdresser's,
or anywhere else where there are a lot of mirrors
– a vampire's lack of a reflection is guaranteed to cause
widespread panic.

The whole lack-of-reflection thing may also mean that
your friend looks a little ungroomed. Find tactful ways of
pointing out any appearance blunders, such as bad-hair
days or cabbage between their front teeth.

Eating out can be a problem – avoid ordering garlic
bread. Vampires hate garlic and will run screaming
from it, causing an embarrassing scene. As your friend

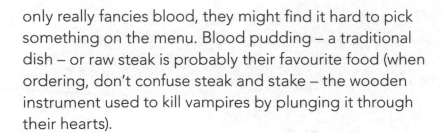

only really fancies blood, they might find it hard to pick something on the menu. Blood pudding – a traditional dish – or raw steak is probably their favourite food (when ordering, don't confuse steak and stake – the wooden instrument used to kill vampires by plunging it through their hearts).

If you cut your finger while carving your meal, beware. The smell of blood will drive your friend crazy and could put them off their pudding.

Party Time

If you invite your vampire friend to your birthday party, there are certain things to remember. Don't ask them to help you blow up the balloons before your party – they are dead and have no breath.

Make sure you answer the door when they arrive – vampires can only come in to your house if they are invited. If someone else answers the doorbell, there could be confusion and delay.

Don't ask your vampire pal to pose with your possie for photos – their image cannot be captured on film.

If you are throwing a party specially for your undead friend, avoid baking a birthday cake. Vampires survive for hundreds of years and your pal might feel self-conscious if you try to fit 207 candles on the cake.

How To Blow The Biggest Bubblegum Bubble

Put a piece of bubblegum in your mouth and chew it well. The larger the piece of gum, the larger the bubble you can blow. Make sure it is soft and stretchy.

With your tongue, flatten the bubblegum across the backs of your top and bottom front teeth.

Using your tongue again, push the centre of the gum out between your teeth. Seal your lips all around the bulge in the gum. Finally, blow into the bulge of bubblegum, and see how big you can get your bubble before it pops and sticks all over your face and hair!

HOW TO COME TOP IN SPELLING TESTS

The English language is difficult to spell because it doesn't follow a simple set of rules (well, not always). The 'spellchecker' you might have on your computer won't be any use to you in an exam or spelling test. There are no magic shortcuts to becoming a good speller, but here are some top tips.

▸ Read as much as you can – books, newspapers, comics, anything you can get your hands on. Take notice of the 'shape' of words on the page, so you will recognize if they are written incorrectly. If you come across a word that you've never seen written down before, try to memorize it.

▸ Follow the 'Look, Think, Cover, Write, Check' procedure: look at the word and think about it, then cover it up and see if you can write it out from memory – then check what you've written.

▸ Word games are great for improving your spelling. Play games such as Hangman, and tackle crosswords and word searches.

▸ Learn spelling rules, such as 'i before e except after c', but remember the exceptions, too. (There are always exceptions to every rule – with this rule they include neighbour, height and weird.)

▸ If you keep getting particular words wrong, why not make up a mnemonic (memory aid) to help you spell it? For example, remember 'There's A RAT in sepARATe'.

A Quick Test

If you want to give someone a hard spelling test, try these:

1. Consensus   **5.** Inoculate   **9.** Supersede

2. Embarrass   **6.** Liaison   **10.** Unnecessary

3. Focused   **7.** Liquefy

4. Foreign   **8.** Phlegm

How To Make A Delicious Breakfast In Bed

If you want to give your mum or dad a really special treat – perhaps for Mothers' Day or Fathers' Day – breakfast in bed is guaranteed to please.

You Will Need:
- a tray
- a pretty tea towel
- crockery and cutlery
- a napkin
- muesli
- milk
- different kinds of fruit
- plain yogurt
- a glass
- fruit juice
- toast
- butter
- jam or honey
- tea or coffee
- a single flower.

What You Do
1. Make your breakfast tray look as good as possible by lining it with a pretty tea towel (this will also make the items on the tray less likely to slip). Use the nicest crockery, cutlery, napkin and glass that you're allowed to get your hands on.

2. Add a bowl of muesli with a small jug of milk next to it. If your mum or dad isn't keen on muesli, make them a fruit salad instead. Chop any of the following fruits you can find in to a bowl – a banana, an apple, a tangerine and some raspberries, strawberries or blueberries. Add a dollop of plain yogurt on top.

3. Fill a glass with fruit juice and add that to the tray, too.

4. Toast a slice or two of bread, and cut them in half diagonally. Put the toast triangles on a plate, together with a small pat of butter and a jar of jam or honey.

5. Don't forget a cup of breakfast tea, herbal tea, or coffee (make sure there is enough milk in the jug for your parent to add some to their hot drink).

6. Add a flower as a fabulous finishing touch.

Top Tip. Your mum or dad might also love a newspaper or a favourite magazine to go with their breakfast.

HOW TO PUT TOGETHER THE BEST DANCE ROUTINES

It takes quite a while to memorize all the moves in a whole dance routine, so allow plenty of time to practise before your performance.

Here are some tips on how to put together a delightful dance routine to wow your friends and family.

▸ Pick a song you love and write down all the lyrics. Break the lyrics down into groups of four lines. Think of dance moves to go with each group of lines and write them down. Watch music videos for inspiration.

▸ Start by working out the basic footwork for each move. Then add some arm and head movements. One move should flow naturally into another, so think about how your body is positioned at the end of a move, and how to get into position for the beginning of the next move.

▸ If you're dancing with a group of friends, make sure everyone can do the moves. Keeping it simple is better than getting it wrong.

▸ Think about where everyone should stand – you don't want someone to be hidden at the back, behind everyone else, where no one can see them strut their stuff.

Make sure you warm up before each practice session. Stretch out your muscles when you've finished.

HOW TO MAKE STALACTITES AND STALAGMITES

Stalactites and stalagmites look like stone icicles that hang from cave ceilings or rise from cave floors, and are formed by water dripping through limestone. With some basic supplies and patience, you can make one.

You Will Need:
- 2 glass jars or plastic cups
- some newspaper
- hot water
- Epsom salts or bicarbonate of soda
- a spoon
- 3 plastic plates
- 2 paperclips
- a 75cm length of wool (or cotton string).

What You Do
1. Find somewhere you can leave your experiment for at least a week without someone tidying it up. It can be messy, so don't use a surface that's easily damaged, and put down several layers of newspaper before you start.

2. Carefully fill one jar about three-quarters full with hot water. Add a few spoonfuls of Epsom salts or bicarbonate of soda, and stir until they are dissolved. Keep adding more salt or soda until no more will dissolve. Now do the same with the second jar.

You could add food colouring to your salt or soda solutions and create coloured stalactites and stalagmites.

3. Stand each jar on a plate on the newspaper, about 20 centimetres apart. Place another plate in between them.

4. Dip the wool or string into one of the jars. Fold the wool in half lengthways and twist it. Attach a paperclip to each end of the twisted wool.

5. Put either end of the wool into each of the jars, as shown below. Let it sag in the middle so that it dangles a few centimetres above the middle plate.

6. Leave your experiment alone for a few days, until your homemade stalactites and stalagmites form on the middle plate.

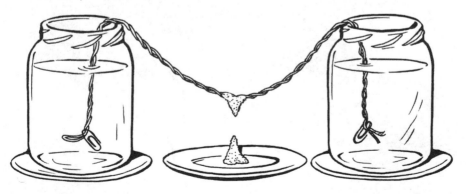

HOW TO MAKE HAND SHADOWS

Stun your friends and family with these amazing hand shadows. To achieve the maximum 'Wow!' effect perform your shadow show in a darkened room with a white or light-coloured wall. Aim a powerful desk lamp at the wall and position your hands in front of it. You could even get a friend in on the act.

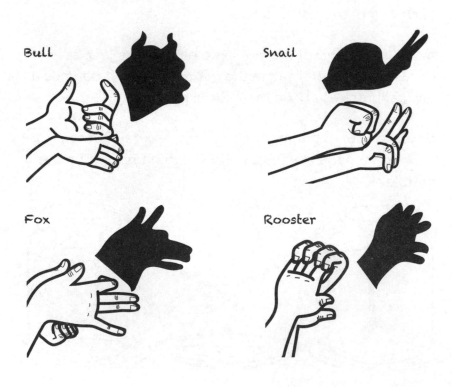

Bull

Snail

Fox

Rooster

Native American

Elephant

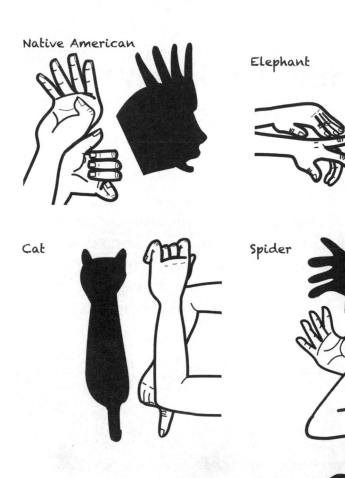

Cat

Spider

Swan

How To Survive An Avalanche

S now avalanches occur when the snow on a mountain slope becomes so heavy that all it wants to do is travel downhill. Every year people perish under tonnes of sliding snow. So if you go skiing or snowboarding, you need to know how to avoid being caught out – especially since most avalanches are caused by the weight of a single person on unstable snow. Here are some tips:

Be Prepared
▸ Be alert. Before you hit the slopes, listen to the radio or TV for avalanche warnings in the area you are in.

▸ On the slopes, look out for recent heavy snowfall and strong winds, rapid changes in temperature, cracks in the snow, and snow that sounds hollow. Avalanches are more likely to happen on steep, north-facing slopes. You might want to avoid them altogether.

▸ Always carry a mobile phone to call for help, and an avalanche beacon – this is a piece of equipment that will tell rescuers where you are.

Emergency Tactics

▸ Once you spot an avalanche speeding towards you, you need to act fast. Don't try to outrun the snow – the snow can travel at great speeds.

▸ Drop all your ski poles as they may injure you when you fall. As the snow surrounds you, try to stay near the top of it by 'swimming' upwards towards the surface. Try to grab a tree or bush if you slide past them.

▸ As the avalanche slows down, curl your body into a ball with your hands over your face. When you stop moving, quickly move your hands back and forwards to make an air space in front of your face with your hands. The snow sets hard within seconds, so this is very important.

▸ Turn on your avalanche beacon and sit tight – help is on the way.

HOW TO MAKE A POP-UP CARD

This flower card is very easy to make and it looks amazing. It's perfect for Mothers' Day or a friend's birthday.

You Will Need:
- an A4 sheet of coloured paper
- scissors
- a glue stick
- pens.

What You Do

1. Fold the paper in half lengthways, then fold the top layer in half again.

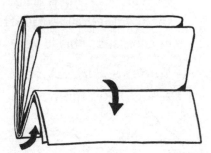

2. Cut down the two fold marks you have made and you will have three strips of paper – one wide and two narrow.

3. Take one of the narrow strips and fold it in half so the short ends are together. Then fold it in half twice more, so you have a small rectangle, eight layers thick.

4. Make one final fold, to find the centre of the rectangle, then open it out and round off the top corners with your scissors. Make a small notch in the centre to complete your petal shape.

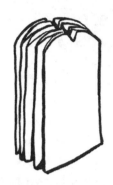

5. Repeat steps **3** and **4** with the other narrow strip.

6. Make four notches in the top of one strip, and four notches in the bottom of the other strip, as shown here. Then slot the strips together, so that they weave in and out.

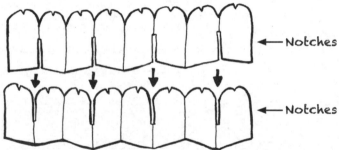

Notches

Notches

7. Starting at one end of the strip, flatten out the pairs of petals so that you end up with eight pairs of petals side by side.

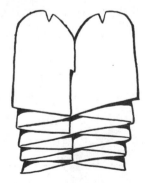

8. Take the wide strip of paper – cut it in half along the width and discard one piece. Fold the remaining piece in half – this is the outside of your pop-up card.

9. Place your petals in the centre of the card and put a dab of glue at each point shown here. Close the card over it and press firmly.

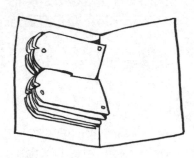

10. Turn the card over and repeat on the other side. Once dry, open your card out to reveal the pretty pop-up flower.

11. Now use felt-tip pens to decorate the front of the card with your greeting – 'Happy Birthday', or 'Happy Mothers' Day', for instance.

> If you're going to give the card as a surprise, try to make it in secret, so that person receiving the card doesn't know about it.

How To Do A Quick Card Trick

Amaze your friends with this quick card trick. They'll never be able to guess how you did it! Just remember, practice makes perfect, so don't perform the trick in public until you've given it a go in private first.

1. Shuffle a deck of cards. Peek at the bottom card and remember it.

2. Ask your friend to pick any card, memorize it, but not show you.

3. Cut the deck. Hold out the top half of the deck and ask your friend to put their card on top of it.

4. Place the bottom half of the deck on top of the top half.

5. Tap the deck mysteriously. Then turn over the cards, one by one. When you come to the card you saw at the bottom of the pack, you'll know your friend's card is the next card.

How To Make
A Step-Pyramid Cake

This cake makes an ideal centrepiece for an
Egyptian-themed party – it's simply fit for a pharaoh.

You Will Need:
Important Note. The quantities listed below make one
square cake. You will need to make three cakes in order to
create your pyramid, so you need to have three times all
ingredients listed.

- 200g butter
- 200g caster sugar
- 4 eggs
- 1 teaspoon vanilla essence
- 200g self-raising flour
- 100g plain flour
- jam
- whipped cream
- icing sugar.

What You Do
1. Preheat the oven to 160°C (Gas Mark 3), and grease
and line a 20-centimetre square cake tin.

2. Mix the butter and sugar together vigorously with a
wooden spoon until it's light and fluffy.

3. Add one egg and stir the mixture thoroughly. Repeat
until all four eggs have been added, one by one. Then stir
in the vanilla essence.

4. Sift the self-raising and plain flour together in a separate bowl, then gently mix it into the egg, butter and sugar mixture.

5. Pour the mixture into your lined cake tin. Bake it in the centre of the oven for about 75 minutes. You can check the cake is ready by putting a skewer into the middle of the cake – it should come out clean.

> **Warning.** Always wear oven gloves when putting something in the oven or taking it out. Get an adult to help you.

6. Take the cake out of the oven, remove it from the tin and leave it to cool on a wire rack.

7. Make two more cakes like this one, using the same method.

To Make The Pyramid

1. The first cake will form the base of your pyramid. Place it in the centre of a cake board.

2. For the next layer, trim 4cm of cake from the length and width of another cake, so that you are left with a cake measuring 16cm by 16cm. Spread one side of the square with a layer of jam and carefully stick it in the centre of the first layer.

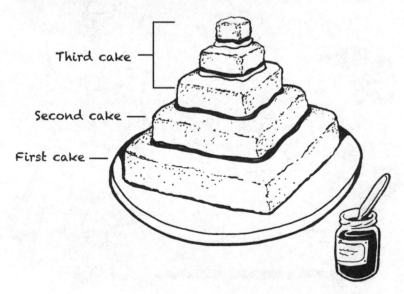

Third cake

Second cake

First cake

3. The final square cake makes several layers. First cut one square which measures 12cm by 12cm. Spread one side with jam and place it in the centre of the first two layers.

4. From the remaining cake, cut another square, measuring 8cm by 8cm, and one measuring 4cm by 4cm. Spread each square with jam and cream, and place them one after the other on top of your pyramid.

Finishing Touches
Using a sieve, sprinkle icing sugar all over your pyramid – in Egyptian times, some pyramids were covered in a layer of white limestone which made them glisten in sunlight.

You have made an Egyptian step pyramid!

Why not have an Egyptian-themed party and dress up as Cleopatra? You could all make Egyptian-style collars, and you could decorate the room with hieroglyphics and Egyptian-inspired designs.

How To Survive An Alien Invasion

Aliens usually invade large cities where they can cause maximum death and destruction, so when news of an invasion first breaks consider moving to the countryside.

▸ Alien spaceships are very large and hard to miss. This gives you an advantage. If, in the middle of the day, the sun is suddenly blocked out and there is no eclipse scheduled in your area, take immediate action and alert the authorities.

▸ Stockpile enough food and water to keep your family alive for several weeks and barricade yourself in your house.

▸ Aliens are supremely intelligent beings, but they often have trouble with simple things such as doorknobs, or going up and down stairs. So hide in the largest upstairs room in your house. Aliens are also easily confused by their own reflection, so line the room with every mirror you can find in the house.

▸ Alien spacecraft often have a disastrous effect on electrical circuits, so don't rely on your parent's car to get away.

▸ Make sure your bike has plenty of air in the tyres in case you need to use it in an emergency.

▸ Aliens will sometimes try to disguise themselves as humans. Luckily they are not very good at it. If you come across an incredibly short man with glowing red eyes and a strange, echoing voice, trust your instincts and run away as fast as you can.

▸ Alien races often have fatal reactions to things that are commonplace on earth, such as water or the cold virus. If you come face-to-face with a creature from another planet, try squirting it with a water pistol or sneezing on it.

How To Host Your Own Awards Ceremony

Whether you've done super-well in your exams or if you fancy celebrating your friends' achievements, why not host an awards ceremony, complete with a red carpet?

Invitations And Envelopes

Design some invitations to the ceremony. Use metallic pen to write them – gold lettering on white card looks particularly stylish. The invite should include the date, time and the venue of the ceremony. Make sure the invites are posted out to your pals with plenty of time to spare.

You need to decide on the different categories you are going to present awards for. They need to be suited to your friends' talents and could include – Best Friend in Need, Greenest Friend, Greatest Gift to the Eyeliner Industry, Coolest Geek, Best Karaoke Performance. Make sure everyone invited to the ceremony can win at least one category.

Decorate envelopes for each category. Put the name of the category and the names of three friends who have been nominated for the award on the front. Slip a piece of paper naming the winner inside.

Warn all your guests that they should prepare a dazzling yet tearful acceptance speech, thanking everyone they've ever met in case they win an award. Remind them that they should also practise smiling convincingly and clapping loudly if someone else wins the award they are nominated for.

Setting The Scene

You'll need awards to hand out. These could be cardboard 'Oscars', or certificates you've designed and printed yourself. You could even give out little gifts, such as a chocolate bar, your friend's favourite magazine or a bunch of flowers.

Finally, find a length of cheap, red fabric – scour charity shops for old red curtains or a bright red duvet cover – to act as a red carpet outside the entrance to your house.

And The Winner Is …
On the night of the award ceremony, get all your friends to dress up in their best dresses, with as much bling as possible. As they walk up the 'red carpet', get someone in your family to take a few photos – this may be the closest to the paparazzi they ever come. You can choose the best one to give them as a souvenir later.

Hand each friend one category envelope to present at the ceremony – but make sure there's no peeking inside.

Start the proceedings by presenting the first category award yourself. Put on an Oscar-worthy performance to show your mates how it is done and present the award with a flourish.

Choose another member of your family to be in charge of the music. They need to switch it on when someone goes up to receive an award and again when they leave. They must turn it down during acceptance speeches and turn it on full blast if a speech gets dull to encourage that person to leave the stage.

Remember – it's all showbiz!

HOW TO TEACH YOUR CAT TO SIT

Many people think our feline friends are impossible to train, but you really can teach your cat to sit.

What You Do

1. Before you start, make sure your cat is feeling relaxed and happy. Stroke it to make it feel comfortable.

2. Show your cat an edible treat (such as a cat biscuit) and say, 'Fluffy [use your cat's name], sit!'

3. Move the treat back over the cat's head. As it watches the treat it should sit down to balance – if it doesn't, gently press down on its hind quarters.

4. As it sits, give lots of praise, and the treat.

Given time, your cat will learn that when it sits it gets the treat, and it'll do it without you moving it over its head. Be patient and keep practising. If you find that either you or the cat is becoming frustrated, leave it 'til another time.

How To Count In Roman Numerals

The Romans were good at lots of things, but they had a very awkward number system. If you were an ancient Roman, this is what you could have had to contend with:

$$
\begin{aligned}
\text{I (Unus)} &= 1 \\
\text{V (Quinque)} &= 5 \\
\text{X (Decem)} &= 10 \\
\text{L (Quinquaginta)} &= 50 \\
\text{C (Centum)} &= 100 \\
\text{D (Quingenti)} &= 500 \\
\text{M (Mille)} &= 1{,}000
\end{aligned}
$$

All the numbers in between are written with these numerals, too. For example, numbers 1, 2 and 3 are I, II and III.

If there's a smaller numeral in front of a larger one, this means you subtract the smaller number from the larger one. So:

IV	=	5 minus 1	=	4
IX	=	10 minus 1	=	9
XL	=	50 minus 10	=	40
VC	=	100 minus 5	=	95

A larger numeral followed by a smaller one means you should add the numbers together. For example:

VII	=	5 plus 2	=	7
XVI	=	10 plus 5 plus 1	=	16
LX	=	50 plus 10	=	60
CLV	=	100 plus 50 plus 5	=	155

Bigger numbers can be shown by adding a line on top of a numeral, which multiplies it by 1,000. For example:

$$\overline{V} = 5,000$$
$$\overline{L} = 50,000$$
$$\overline{C} = 100,000$$
$$\overline{M} = 1,000,000$$

If you think all this is confusing, try multiplication and long division using Roman numerals!

How To Make Sure Your Trainers Smell Good

Here are some fool-proof ways of avoiding those embarrassing moments when you sit back, kick off your shoes and your friends kick up a fuss. These techniques are guaranteed to ensure you have the sweetest-smelling trainers around.

▸ Stuff several unused tea bags into each shoe and leave for a couple of days.

 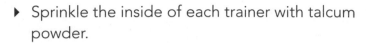
- Sprinkle the inside of each trainer with talcum powder.

- Drip a couple of drops of essential oil on the inner soles. Try tea tree, rose or peppermint oil.

- Fill two clean socks with cat litter (ideally some that your cat hasn't already used), and leave them in your trainers overnight.

- Tuck sheets of a fabric-softener in to the bottom of your trainers, underneath the inner soles.

HOW TO KEEP A SECRET DIARY

Would you like somewhere to write your hopes and dreams, and deepest, darkest secrets? Are you afraid that if you do, someone will find it and read it? Well here are a few pointers on how to keep your secret diary just that … a secret.

- Don't tell anyone that you are writing a diary. If they don't know you keep one, they will not go looking for it. Frequently make comments like, 'Diaries are so stupid.'

▸ Disguise your diary by wrapping the dust jacket of a story book around it. Pop your camouflaged diary on a shelf with your other books.

▸ Write 'My Diary' on the cover of an old notebook, add a few really boring entries and leave it lying around.

▸ In your real diary, make up code words for people and places. Anyone who finds it will be unable to understand what you've written. Write your code down if you need to, but keep it hidden in a different place to your diary.

▸ Write a few completely far-fetched entries like, 'Yesterday, I met a three-legged woman out shopping for shoes.' That way, anyone who reads it will not know what is true and what is made up.

HOW TO SPEAK 'PIRATE'

Avast thar, landlubbers. So, ye be wantin' to speak like a pirate? Yarr! First, you'll be learnin' some pirate vocabulary, then you'll be discoverin' yer own true pirate name.

Pirate Vocabulary

▸ Ahoy ... Hello

▸ Avast ... Stop

▸ Bilge rat ... Rat that lives in the lowest, slimiest part of the ship – used as an insult

▸ Booty ... Treasure

▸ Cat o' nine tails ... Whip used in seafaring punishment

▸ Davy Jones's locker ... The bottom of the ocean

▸ Doubloons ... Gold pieces

▸ Fiddler's Green ... Pirate heaven

▸ Galley ... Kitchen

▸ Grog ... Alcoholic drink

▸ Hearty ... Friend (as in 'me hearty')

- Hornswaggler … Cheat

- Jolly Roger … Pirate flag

- Keelhauling … Dragging someone along the bottom of the ship as a punishment

- Landlubber … Someone not used to life at sea ('land lover')

- Matey … Friend/shipmate

- Pieces of eight … Silver coins cut into eight pieces

- Scurvy dog/Scurvy cur … Sick dog, used as an insult

- Shiver me timbers! … Exclamation of surprise

- Walkin' the plank … Making someone walk on to a plank and off the side of the ship, preferably into shark-infested waters, as punishment

- Yarr! … General exclamation, usually positive.

Your Pirate Name

Add a tenth name to each of the columns below. Then choose three numbers between 1 and 10, and look up the three names that correspond to those numbers – choose one from each of the three columns. Put the three names together and you'll have your pirate name. Get your friends to do it, too.

1.	Captain	Bess	Blackheart
2.	Crazy	Kate	Flint
3.	First Mate	Peg	Morgan
4.	Bloodthirsty	Mary	Cutlass
5.	Ruthless	Mags	Kidd
6.	Stinky	Ann	Bonny
7.	Peg-leg	Flora	Finnegan
8.	Fearless	Nell	Silver
9.	Daring	Pearl	Braveheart
10.			

My pirate name is ....

HOW TO DO FINGER KNITTING

Finger knitting uses the same techniques as knitting with needles. Try finger knitting first, then move on to using needles when you feel more confident. Use the following finger-knitting method to make a long strip of knitting to wear as a hairband.

1. Get a ball of wool. Wrap the end of the wool loosely around the index finger of your left hand (or right hand if you are left-handed) and tie a knot in it. The loose end of the wool should be hanging down the back of your hand.

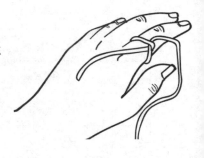

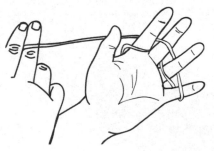

2. Weave the working end of the wool (the bit attached to the ball) behind your middle finger, in front of your ring finger and then behind your little finger. Make sure the loops are not too tight.

3. Now weave back to your index finger, so the wool goes in front of your little finger, behind the ring finger, and so on. Then repeat steps **2** and **3**, so you have two strands of wool on each finger. The second weave of wool should lie above the first weave.

4. Starting at your little finger, lift the bottom loop of wool over the top loop. Slip it off your finger and drop it behind your hand. Repeat with the bottom loop on your ring finger. Continue in this way until all four fingers have only one strand of wool wrapped around them.

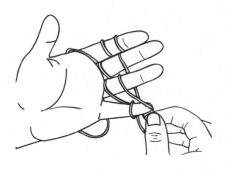

5. Start weaving, so you have two strands around each finger. Then repeat step **4**. Keep going until you have a knitted strip behind your hand long enough to go around your head if you are making a knitted hairband.

6. To finish, make sure you are at a point where there is only one strand of wool on each finger. Lift the loop off your little finger. Slip it on to your ring finger, so that this finger holds two strands of wool.

7. Lift the bottom strand on your ring finger over the top one and slip it off your finger. Drop it behind your hand. Lift the remaining loop off your ring finger and slip it on to your middle finger. Repeat until you are left with one strand on your index finger. Cut the wool off the ball, leaving a 15 centimetre tail. Feed the tail through the remaining loop. Slip it off your finger and pull it tight to secure the end of your knitting.

HOW TO SHOW OFF YOUR SUPERHUMAN STRENGTH

Impress your friends by telling them you have the powers of a superhero. They won't believe you, but you can prove it with this easy but amazing trick. Your friends won't believe their eyes.

1. Hold a full-sized umbrella horizontally in front of you so that it is level with your shoulders and about

25 centimetres away from your body. Your elbows should be bent at all times, so that they are almost at right angles.

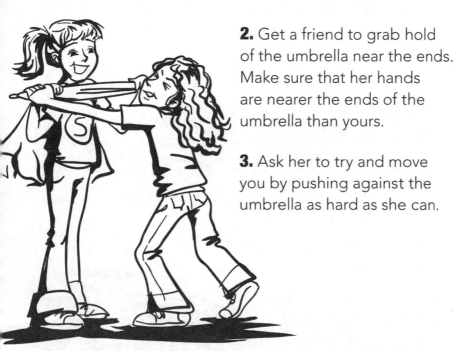

2. Get a friend to grab hold of the umbrella near the ends. Make sure that her hands are nearer the ends of the umbrella than yours.

3. Ask her to try and move you by pushing against the umbrella as hard as she can.

4. As she pushes, push upwards to keep the umbrella in position. This deflects the pressure upwards rather than against your body and your friend will not be able to budge you.

To make this an even more impressive feat, you can ask another friend to add her weight, by standing behind the first person and pushing against her shoulders. You should be able to resist them both.

How To Survive In A Horror Movie

Should you ever find yourself in a horror-movie type situation, which is, let's face it, extremely unlikely, there are some basic rules you should follow to make sure you escape unscathed.

▸ When it appears that you have killed a monster, never approach it to check if it's really dead – it will pounce on you.

▸ When running away from a monster expect to fall over at least twice.

▸ If your car breaks down at night, don't go to a deserted-looking mansion to phone for help.

▸ Never accept invitations from strangers who live in isolated areas and have no contact with society.

▸ Do not search the basement – especially if the lights have just gone out and the phone is dead.

▸ If your date has fangs, go home.

▸ If your date has rotting green flesh and behaves more like a zombie than most dates, go home.

▸ Never, ever say 'I'll be right back.' You won't be.

How To Dust For Fingerprints

Do you need to carry out your own crime-scene investigation? Dusting for prints could reveal who's been at the biscuit jar, or who sneaked a peek at your top-secret diary.

You Will Need:
- some fine powder (talcum powder or cocoa powder work well)
- a paintbrush
- some clear sticky tape
- a piece of card
- an inked stamp pad
- a piece of paper.

Lifting Prints

1. Taking an imprint of fingerprints using the technique described below is known as 'lifting' prints. Fingerprints are hard to lift from a grainy surface like wood, so look for some that have been left on a smooth, shiny surface, such as a mirror or a glass.

2. Very gently, and as evenly as possible, brush some powder over the surface of the prints with your paintbrush. Blow away any excess.

3. If you have revealed several fingerprints, choose the clearest one. Cut a length of sticky tape and cover the print with it, sticky side down. Smooth the tape down all over the print area, before carefully lifting it up with the print underneath.

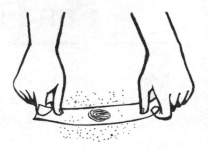

4. Stick the tape containing your print on to some card. If you've used cocoa powder, choose white card. If you've used talc, choose a dark-coloured card.

Selecting Suspects

Now you need to work out whose fingerprint you have lifted. This will mean taking prints from all of your suspects. Take your inked stamp pad and white paper.

Have a suspect gently roll each of his or her fingertips on the stamp pad, then roll the inky fingertips on to some white paper. If you gently hold the tip of each finger down while it is rolling, this will make the print less likely to smudge.

When you have fingerprinted everyone capable of the crime, use a magnifying glass to compare their fingerprints to the one you have lifted. Can you discover a perfect match and catch the culprit?

HOW TO MAKE A PHOTO FRAME

If you have a photograph you love, why not create a special frame for it?

You Will Need:

- 2 pieces of thick card (old cardboard boxes are good)
- a pencil
- a ruler
- scissors
- newspaper
- a mixture of 100ml water and 100ml PVA glue
- a paintbrush
- extra glue
- poster paint

- decorations, such as fake jewels, shells, sweets, cake decorations or dried flowers
- a sheet of clear acetate (available from stationers)
- sticky tape.

What You Do

1. Place the photo you want to frame on a piece of card and draw around it. Draw another square inside the first one, about half a centimetre narrower on each side.

2. Draw another square outside the first two, making sure the first two squares are right in the middle. This will be the part of the frame you see, so make it as big as you like.

3. Cut out the smallest and the largest square. You should be left with a frame of cardboard. (Ask an adult to help with cutting out the centre, as this can be a bit tricky.)

4. On another piece of card, draw around the outside of your frame. Cut the square out to form the back of your frame.

5. To give your frame some depth, tear a newspaper into strips, and dip the pieces in the PVA-glue-and-water mixture. Cover the frame with them. Wait until they dry, then add another layer of strips. Repeat until you have added four layers.

6. When your final layer of newspaper is completely dry, paint over it with the diluted glue and leave it to dry overnight.

7. Now paint your photo frame.

8. Arrange your chosen decorations on the frame, then glue them into place. Choose decorations to suit the subject of the photo. When they are stuck in place, cover with undiluted PVA glue to seal them and make them shine.

9. Cut a square out of the sheet of clear acetate at least 1 centimetre larger on each side than the window in your frame. Make a crease in the bottom edge of the acetate (for your photo to sit in), then use sticky tape to secure it on the reverse side of the frame with the bottom flap sticking out.

10. Attach the back of your frame to the reverse of the front, gluing it on three sides, leaving the top side of the frame open.

11. Slip your photo into the frame and position it in the window.

HOW TO LOOK AFTER BABY CHICKS

1. Find a cage that is large enough for the chicks. Each one will need at least 40cm² of space. Cover the bottom of the cage with 2½ centimetres of wood shavings.

2. Chicks need to be kept warm. You will need a special 250-watt light bulb. This will provide enough heat for 50 chicks. The light bulb should be about 45 centimetres above the bottom of the cage.

3. Make sure that part of the cage is sheltered from the heat of the bulb, so the chicks can move there if they get too hot. Keep draughts out by covering the outside of the cage with cardboard.

4. Teach the chicks where to go for food by sprinkling some of their feed underneath the feeder.

5. Frequently check that the chicks have enough water. Dip each chick's beak into the water when you place it in the cage to let them know it is there.

HOW TO TRAIN A DOG TO SHAKE HANDS

Anyone can teach their dog to sit or come to them, but shaking hands shows the world that you and your dog are pedigree chums.

You can start training your dog when it is about 12 weeks old. Always be patient when training. You should be firm and authoritative, but never shout at or hit your dog.

1. Get your dog to sit down in front of you. Praise him when he obeys and offer him a tasty treat.

2. Gently pick up one of his front paws and hold it loosely in your hand, saying 'Shake' as you do so.

3. Reward your dog immediately with a treat and repeat this exercise several times.

4. Next, put your hand out and give the command 'Shake'. Give your dog the chance to put his paw on your open palm as you repeat the command. If he doesn't do it after a couple of seconds, pick up his paw while saying 'Shake'.

5. Keep at it – you will get there in the end.

How To Be A Great Magician

Every great magician knows that the secret of success is thorough preparation. Here are some golden rules for slick and faultless performances. Get ready to take the stage …

- ▸ Practise every trick you perform again and again until you can do it in your sleep. Rehearse in front of a mirror. This way you'll be able to see what your audience sees.

- ▸ Run through what you will say while performing your tricks. A good, amusing commentary distracts your audience's attention just enough to keep them puzzling over how a magic trick is performed.

▸ Never perform a trick twice in front of the same audience, even if they beg you to. Never reveal how a trick is done.

▸ Set up the chairs your audience will sit on before a show begins – many tricks require the people to be looking directly at you so they can't see around the back of you.

▸ Whenever possible borrow props, such as coins and pencils, from your audience – that way they will know that the items are completely genuine.

How To Make Quick Icy Milkshakes

Here's a super-speedy way of making mouth-watering icy milkshakes, guaranteed to have people begging for more.

1. Pour a cup of milk into a plastic food bag that can be sealed and add a tablespoon of sugar and a few drops of vanilla essence. Seal the bag tightly and then give it a good shake to mix up the ingredients.

2. Fill a larger plastic bag with ice cubes. Place the bag containing the milkshake mix inside the larger plastic bag and tie a tight knot in the top.

3. Shake the bag for five minutes. Be careful because water will leak out of the bag, so it is a good idea to do this bit outside.

4. Remove the small bag, open it carefully and enjoy.

Use the same technique to make sorbets, adding water and fruit juice instead of milk and vanilla.

How To Make A Time Capsule

Let future generations know all about you and the world you live in. Find a container that can be sealed to protect its contents. A plastic storage container is ideal. Write, 'Not to be opened until the year 2030,' or whatever date you like, on the outside. Here are some things to put in the capsule.

▸ A letter or a recording addressed to the person who finds your capsule. State today's date and tell them a bit about yourself and your life. You could describe what you imagine the future will be like.

▸ Some photographs of you and your family.

▸ This week's issue of your favourite magazine.

▸ A CD of your favourite songs.

▸ A shiny new coin minted this year.

▸ Don't include anything valuable or edible.

When the container is full, bury it or put it in your loft.

HOW TO TELL IF SOMEONE IS TELLING THE TRUTH

It's impossible to know for sure whether a friend is being honest or telling a great big fib, but there are some classic tell-tale signs you can look out for to help you decide:

▸ A guilty person will often speak more than they do normally, adding lots of unnecessary details in an attempt to convince you of what they are saying. Look out for this or for your friend talking to avoid uncomfortable silences or pauses in the conversation.

▸ Is she touching her face, or tugging at her ear or hair a lot? Fidgeting, blinking and scratching are all signs of an unusual level of nervousness that might be caused by fibbing.

▸ Does your friend keep trying to change the subject? She may do this rather obviously – pointing and saying, 'Oooh! Look over there!' – or she may be more subtle, saying 'Did you watch that film last night?'

▸ You can play this subject-changing game, too. Try changing the subject of a conversation quickly yourself – if your pal is a fibber she will be glad and look more relaxed. An innocent person may look confused by your sudden change of topic.

▸ Is your friend covering her mouth, nose or throat with her hand? This is a classic clue that she wants to hide her fibs.

▸ When people are trying to recall a piece of information they are more likely to raise their eyes up and to the left. If they are trying to make something up, they're more likely to look up and to the right. Look out for these odd eye movements.

▸ Avoiding eye contact is a well-known sign that someone isn't telling the truth. Many people know this, and someone telling a lie might try to make lots of eye contact to fool you. Look out for either a lack of eye contact or more than usual.

> **Warning.** These traits are just guidelines. Just because your friend may behave in a few of the ways described above, it doesn't mean she is lying. Don't let your suspicions lead you to accuse her, as it could hurt her feelings.

How To Make Chocolate Pecan Fudge

Create these delicious, chocolatey treats to give as a gift, serve at a party, or simply keep all to yourself.

You Will Need:
- 450g dark chocolate
- 75g unsalted butter (at room temperature)
- 400g tin sweetened condensed milk
- ½ teaspoon vanilla essence
- 100g of chopped pecan nuts
- greased baking parchment
- a 20cm square baking tin.

What You Do

1. Chop the chocolate into squares. Then heat the chocolate, butter and condensed milk together in a saucepan over a low heat until the chocolate melts. Keep stirring and be careful not to let it burn.

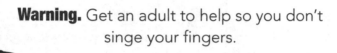

Warning. Get an adult to help so you don't singe your fingers.

2. Take the saucepan off the heat when the chocolate has melted and stir in the vanilla essence.

3. Stir in the chopped pecan nuts.

4. Line a 20-centimetre baking tin with greased baking parchment. Then pour in the mixture and leave it to cool.

5. Put the mixture in the fridge and leave it for an hour, or until it has completely set.

6. Cut the fudge into bite-sized pieces, and wrap each piece in baking parchment until you're ready to eat it.

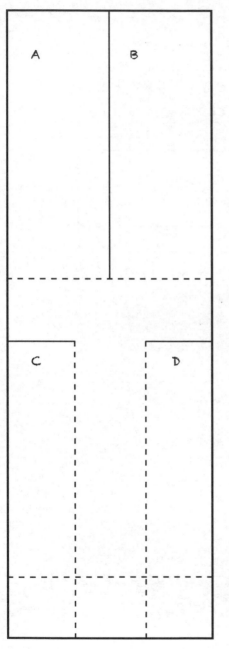

HOW TO FLY A PAPER HELICOPTER

This paper helicopter couldn't be simpler to make, and it's so much more interesting than a paper plane.

You Will Need:
- a sheet of paper
- a pen
- a ruler
- scissors
- a paperclip.

What You Do

1. Trace this design on to the sheet of paper. The solid lines are cut lines and the dotted lines are fold lines.

2. Cut the shape out along the cut lines.

3. Fold along the dotted line 16mm from the bottom.

4. Fold along the dotted line marked **C**.

5. Turn the paper over, fold along the dotted line marked **D**.

6. Slide a paperclip on to the base of your helicopter as shown.

7. Fold flap **A** towards you and flap **B** away from you.

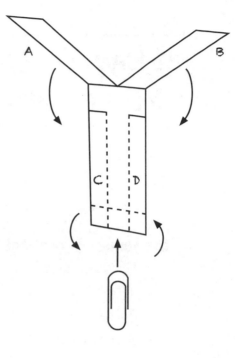

8. Your helicopter is ready to fly. Throw it into the air, paperclip end first, and watch it twirl through the air.

Get your friends to make helicopters and see who can keep theirs in the air longest.

HOW TO CONVINCE PEOPLE YOU'RE AN ANIMAL EXPERT

Here are some facts which, when casually dropped into the conversation, will convince your friends that you are a world authority on the animal kingdom.

Marvellous Movement

▸ Cows can walk up stairs, but not down them.

▸ The longest recorded flight of a chicken is 13 seconds.

▸ A mole can dig a tunnel 90 metres long in a night.

▸ Kangaroos can't walk backwards.

Sleeping Beauties

▸ A snail can go to sleep for three years.

▸ Ants don't sleep.

▸ Dolphins sleep with one eye open.

Noses, Taste And Tongues

▸ Giraffes can clean their ears with their tongues.

▸ Butterflies taste with their feet.

▸ Slugs have four noses.

▸ Crocodiles can't stick their tongues out.

Bonkers And Bizarre

‣ All polar bears are left-handed.

‣ A hedgehog's heart beats an average of 300 times a minute.

‣ A donkey can see all four of its feet at the same time.

‣ Cats have 32 muscles in each ear.

‣ An ostrich's eye is bigger than its brain.

‣ If you cut off a cockroach's head it can survive for weeks until it starves to death.

‣ Sharks don't have bones.

> Make these facts even more impressive by adding phrases such as, 'My sources indicate that …' or 'My research has shown that …' or 'I feel sure that my colleagues would not dispute that …'.

HOW TO SURVIVE A RIP CURRENT

A rip current is an area of water near the surface of the sea that flows rapidly away from shore. They can pull even the strongest swimmers out to sea. Once you know how to deal with them, you should be able to get back to shore safely.

Emergency Tactics

If you are swimming and suddenly realize you are being pulled out to sea by a current, don't panic! It will only make you disorientated – you need to keep a clear head.

Don't try and swim back to shore. You won't be strong enough to swim against the current, and trying to do so will just tire you out. Swim parallel with the line of the beach. If the pull of the current makes this too difficult, just wait until the current takes you into calmer water.

Rip currents are usually no more than about ten metres wide. Once you've swum far enough along, parallel to the beach, you should arrive outside the area affected by the current. Then you should be able to swim back in to shore, or you can let the waves take you back in.

On tourist beaches there are usually signs warning you if the area is prone to dangerous rip currents. Take notice of these warnings and never swim in areas that are marked as unsafe. Always stick to the area of the beach that is patrolled by a trained lifeguard.

Warning. Don't go into the sea on your own, and if you're not a strong swimmer, stay in shallow water.

How To
Walk The Dog

This is a yo-yo trick, not a fun outing for one of your canine pals, and is best performed on a wooden or tiled floor.

1. Hold the yo-yo in your hand with your palm facing upwards. Slip your middle finger through the loop of the string. Make sure the string winds up from your finger over the top of the yo-yo towards your body, in the direction indicated by the arrow.

2. Bend your arm at the elbow, then straighten it. When your arm is almost straight in front of you, flick your wrist, releasing the yo-yo forwards and downwards. Turn your hand palm down and lower your arm as the yo-yo falls. As the yo-yo reaches the ground stop lowering your arm and give the string an upward tug. The yo-yo will climb back up the string to your hand. Catch it.

3. This time, repeat steps **2** to **4**, but as the yo-yo drops downwards let it touch the ground. It will roll along the floor away from you and this is 'walking the dog'.

HOW TO SCORE A NETBALL GOAL

1. The moment the ball is passed to you, turn and line up your body with the goalpost. Check your feet, shoulders and elbows are all pointing towards it. Make sure your feet are planted shoulder-width apart to increase your balance.

2. Take a deep breath, steady yourself and focus on the net. Don't allow the defenders to spoil your concentration.

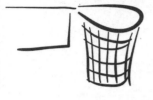

3. Balance the ball on the tips of the fingers of your right hand (the left hand if you are left-handed).

4. Place your other hand on the side of the ball to keep it steady.

> To improve your chances of scoring, spin the ball backwards as you release it by flicking your wrists. This way, if the ball bounces on the rim of the goal it is more likely to go in.

HOW TO MAKE A STAINED-GLASS WINDOW

Follow these instructions to make a beautiful 'stained-glass' window.

1. Take two pieces of black card and two pieces of greaseproof paper all of equal size. Decide on a simple picture, for example a leaf or a dolphin. Sketch your shape on to one piece of card.

2. Hold the two pieces of card neatly together and cut out your shape, leaving a border of card around it.

3. Select wax crayons in the colours you want to decorate your picture. With a sharp craft knife carefully shave the crayons.

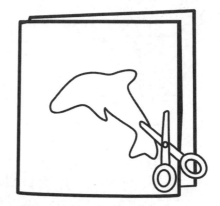

4. Spread the wax shavings on one of the sheets of greaseproof paper. Place the other sheet on top and run a warm iron over them.

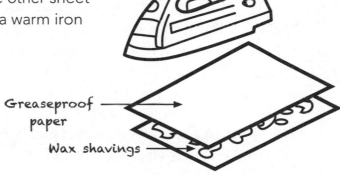

Greaseproof paper

Wax shavings

5. To assemble the window, place one piece of the card flat on a table and glue the sandwich of greaseproof paper to it. Then glue the other piece of card on top, trapping the greaseproof paper between the two pieces of card. Hang your finished work near a window so that the light shines through it.

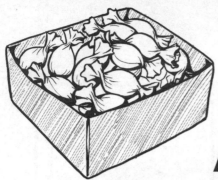

HOW TO MAKE AN ORIGAMI BOX

These little boxes are very cute, as well as being useful for storing paperclips, beads, craft supplies or sweets. They're really easy to make, though you'll find it more difficult with thicker card. All you need is a square piece of paper.

What You Do

1. Fold the paper in half, then open it out and fold it in half the other way. Every time you fold the paper, make a sharp crease.

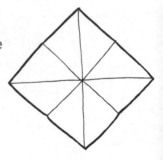

2. Open the paper out again and fold it in half diagonally. Open it out and fold it in half diagonally the other way.

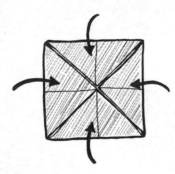

3. Open the paper out and fold all four corners into the centre.

4. Fold two opposite sides into the centre. Open them out again, then fold the other two sides into the centre in the same way, and open out again. These will be the sides of your box.

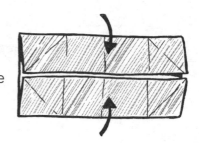

5. Open out two opposite corners, as shown. Push the point at the edge of one of the sides inwards, so that you're reversing the fold. Do the same with the other side.

6. Now bring the point of the flap over, and tuck it around the two reversed folds to make the third side of the box.

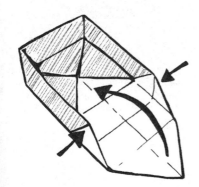

7. Repeat steps **5** and **6** to make the fourth side.

8. To make a lid for your box, repeat steps **1** to **6** with a square of paper, half a centimetre larger than the first in length and width.

HOW TO HOST THE BEST SLEEPOVER

Follow these top tips and you'll soon be known as a duvet diva who hosts the best sleepovers in town.

▸ Invite a maximum of four guests as you want to make sure you have time to give each of them your full attention. Send out hand-made invitations well ahead of time so that you can be sure your friends will be free on the night. Ask your guests to reply so you know how many are coming.

▸ It's a good idea to choose a theme for your sleepover and ask each guest to bring one thing that will contribute to the fun. If you're planning a night of salon-style pampering, for example, they could bring hair straighteners and make-up. Plan activities and decorate your room around the theme.

▸ Think of some games you can play and gather everything you need to play them before your guests arrive. Get your friends to bring their favourite CDs, DVDs or board games.

▸ Be a good hostess — check that everyone has everything they need and knows where the bathroom is. Make sure everyone has somewhere comfortable to sleep (you can ask your guests to bring sleeping bags if necessary).

▸ Provide plenty of food for your pals, including treats for a midnight feast and breakfast.

▸ Make sure everyone sticks to the sacred sleepover rule — secrets told at the sleepover stay at the sleepover.

How To Make A Fake Mess

Freak out your folks with a fake mess that's guaranteed to get you grounded – until they realize it's not real.

You Will Need:

- some paint (in whichever colour you choose to make your mess)
- white craft glue
- greaseproof paper
- some porridge oats (if you make fake sick)
- some props, for example a coffee mug.

1. Decide what kind of mess you want to make – a coffee spill, an ink accident, or how about cat sick on your brother's favourite top?

2. Mix up some paint. A milk-chocolate brown works for coffee, royal blue for ink, and pink and orange is good for sick.

3. Add drops of white craft glue until the paint is thick and sticky.

4. If you want to make the fake sick super-convincing, you should add some porridge to the mixture for extra realism.

5. Pour the paint mixture on to a piece of greaseproof paper and leave it to dry completely.

6. Once the paint has dried, cut round the edges of the paint so none of the greaseproof paper can be seen.

7. Place the mess wherever it will have the best effect, on your dad's favourite tie, on the beautifully polished wooden table. Set up some props, like a coffee mug lying on its side nearby.

8. Now simply wait for someone to come along, spot it and shriek!

How To Make A Fake Fossil

It's not difficult to make fake fossils that would be worthy of any palaeontologist's collection. (A palaeontologist is someone who studies fossils.) Why not make lots of different fake fossils and create a collection?

You Will Need:
- modelling clay
- an object to fossilize
  – small plastic toy insects, animals or dinosaurs, or a shell or bone
- a paintbrush
- petroleum jelly
- plaster of Paris
- water
- a rolling pin.

What You Do

1. Knead the modelling clay until it's soft, then roll it flat with the rolling pin. Roll it out to about 2 centimetres thick. Make sure it's bigger than the object you want to fossilize.

2. Use the paintbrush to cover the object you want to fossilize with a thin layer of petroleum jelly (this will make it easier to remove from the clay later).

3. Push the object into the clay. Leave it there until the clay is completely dry – 24 hours or so – and then remove it. You now have your fossil mould.

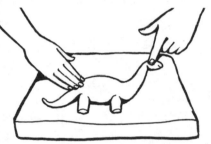

4. To make your cast, you need to make up the plaster of Paris in a plastic container (follow the instructions on the packet).

5. Use your paintbrush to cover the inside of your mould with a thin layer of petroleum jelly. Pour the plaster of Paris into the mould. Leave it to set for at least 30 minutes.

6. Remove the cast and leave it to dry completely.

You now have a cool fake fossil.

HOW TO TRAVEL WITH JUST ONE BAG

The most sophisticated travellers never struggle with loads of bags. Clever packing is the secret to being one of those glamorous girls who breeze through airports and train stations with just one stylish piece of luggage.

Too many bags ...

▸ First, find the right bag. It should be small enough to be allowed on to planes as hand luggage (good luggage shops will know the dimensions), light, easy to carry and distinctive.

▸ Write a list of everything you are going to need, then look over it and ask yourself if there is anything you could possibly live without. Collect each absolutely necessary item and put it on your bed, crossing it off the list as you do so. Take the list on holiday so that you can check you haven't forgotten anything when it's time to return home.

▸ Choose outfits that you can mix-and-match. Wrap your clothes around other items you're taking. Start with the items least likely to crease and work outwards.

▸ Pour toiletries into small bottles and place anything that could leak in a plastic bag.

▸ Pack your underwear into your shoes – this saves space and stops your shoes getting squashed.

▸ Neatly fold all your clothes and pack them into your suitcase, then fill any gaps with socks.

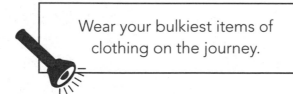
Wear your bulkiest items of clothing on the journey.

HOW TO AVOID JET LAG

If you are flying off on holiday to a different time zone, prepare for your journey three days in advance.

First Day
Eat a high-protein breakfast and lunch, such as bacon, eggs, sausages or steak, and a high-carbohydrate dinner, such as pasta, potatoes or rice.

Second Day
Eat only very light meals.

Third Day
Today you get to eat whatever you want.

Departure Day
As soon as you get on the plane, adjust your watch to the time at your destination. Then make sure you eat meals at your normal times according to your watch. Make sure you also drink lots of water on the flight.

Stay awake during your flight if it is daytime at your destination. Sleep on the plane if it is night-time at your destination. Use earplugs, headphones, and eye masks to block out noise and light.

If you arrive at your destination in the middle of the day, don't go to sleep. Take a shower, go out and do something. In the evening, eat a meal and go to bed at your normal time. Then you should sleep soundly.

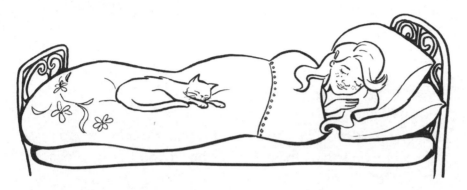

How To Float A Friend

This is an amazing trick. There's no real explanation for why or how it works – it just does. Find five friends willing to take part in your experiment. Choose one friend to be the subject who will be lifted, and ask her to sit on a chair.

1. Ask each of the other four girls to place their hands together, with their palms touching and their fingers outstretched.

2. One girl must place her fingers under the bent left knee of the subject on the chair. Another places her fingers in the same position under the right knee. The third girl places her fingers under one of the subject's armpits, and the fourth girl places their fingers under the other armpit.

3. Tell your friends to try to lift the person up from the chair. Chances are they will fail.

4. Next, ask everyone to stack their hands one on top of the other on top of the subject's head and lightly press down. Tell them to keep pressing while you count to ten, and on the count of ten to quickly get back into their lifting positions and try to lift again – it will work!

HOW TO MAKE SUGAR MICE

S ugar mice are delicious and very easy to make. If you don't eat them all yourself, put some in a decorated box and give them to a friend.

You Will Need:
- an egg
- a cup
- a mixing bowl
- a whisk
- a sieve
- 450g icing sugar
- some lemon juice
- red food colouring
- some string (for the mice's tails)
- edible silver balls (for the mice's eyes)
- a baking tray.

1. Separate the white of an egg from the yolk. To do this, crack the egg carefully over a cup. Tip the yolk of the egg from one half of the egg-shell to the other half, over the cup, until only the yolk is left in the eggshell, and the white has dropped into the cup (you might need to get someone to help as this is quite tricky).

2. Beat the egg white in a mixing bowl with a whisk until it is frothy, but not too stiff.

3. Hold a sieve over the bowl, pour in the icing sugar, sieve it and mix it in. Add drops of lemon juice until the mixture is soft and squidgy.

4. Put a small amount of the mixture into another bowl and add some red food colouring, drop by drop, until the mixture turns pink. You'll use this to make the ears.

5. Take lumps of the white mixture and roll and knead them into the shape of mice.

6. Use tiny amounts of the pink mixture to make ears. Edible silver balls pushed into the icing make great noses and eyes, and you can use pieces of string stuck into the icing to make tails.

7. Place your mice on a baking tray in a cool spot and leave them to set for a couple of hours.

HOW TO KNOW YOUR BIRTH-MONTH FLOWER

There's a special flower (or sometimes two) for every month of the year. If it's the birthday of someone you care about, why not give her a bunch of her birth-month flowers? You could attach a card explaining what the flowers symbolize.

January	Carnation or snowdrop	Love or friendship in hard times
February	Violet or primrose	Faithfulness or love
March	Daffodil	Devotion
April	Daisy or sweetpea	Innocence or goodbye
May	Lily-of-the-valley or hawthorn	Sweetness or hope
June	Rose or honeysuckle	Love
July	Larkspur	Laughter
August	Gladiola	Sincerity
September	Aster	Love
October	Calendula	Happiness
November	Chrysanthemum	Happiness and wealth
December	Poinsettia	Good wishes for the future

HOW TO READ BODY LANGUAGE

Sometimes someone will tell you one thing, but their body language will be 'suggesting' something completely different. Use the list below to work out how people are really feeling.

Biting nails: anxious, insecure

Lounging on chair with arms dangling: relaxed

Clenched jaw, tense muscles: angry

Arms crossed: defensive

Hands clasped behind head: confident

Touching or rubbing nose: rejected, or they are lying

Tapping or drumming fingers: impatient

Patting hair: insecure

Tilted head: interested

Stroking chin: they are making a decision

Pulling at ear: indecisive

Pinching bridge of nose, eyes closed: feeling a sense of foreboding

Looking down, face turned away: a sense of disbelief.

How To Dowse
For Water

Some people claim to be able to detect underground water, and other substances, such as oil or metal, by 'dowsing' for them. Dowsing means locating something that is hidden.

Dowsing rods are used, which cross each other when they come near water. The two L-shaped pieces of metal shown below are made of two bits of wire from a coat hanger, with two lengths of straw threaded on to them to act as handles.

There's no evidence to prove that people really can find water by dowsing, but why not conduct your own experiment with friends?

You Will Need:
- dowsing rods
- some water
- 10 plastic bottles
- 10 buckets or cardboard boxes
- paper and a pen.

What You Do

1. Without any of your friends seeing, fill half the bottles with water and leave the rest empty.

2. Place the bottles about half a metre apart in a row. Cover each with a bucket or box. Number the buckets or boxes clearly.

3. Now ask one of your friends to walk along the row of buckets and tell you if her dowsing rods detect water under any of them. Make a note of which buckets she thinks are covering water and which she thinks are not.

4. When all your friends have done their dowsing, reveal the results.

HOW TO BE
A NATURAL BEAUTY

You can use ingredients you'll find in the fridge and kitchen cupboards to get fresh and healthy-looking skin and hair.

Exfoliate

Mix together a tablespoon of plain yogurt, a drizzle of honey and a teaspoon of granulated sugar. Rub the mixture gently over your face to exfoliate (get rid of dead skin) and to leave your skin glowing. Rinse well.

Eyes

To get rid of dark circles around your eyes, cut a fresh fig in half and place the halves over your eyes for 15 minutes while lying on your bed and relaxing.

For tired eyes, enjoy the cooling effect of two slices of cucumber placed over your eyes. To soothe your eyes, soak cotton pads in rose water, milk or aloe vera juice and place over your lids.

Condition

For smooth silky hair, beat an egg yolk in a bowl, then mix in a teaspoon of olive oil, drip by drip.

Add a cup of warm water. After shampooing, spread the mixture evenly over your hair and leave for a few minutes before rinsing it off. For shiny locks, once a month rinse your hair with a can of flat beer after shampooing. Work it through well before rinsing.

Face Mask

If you have dry skin, mash up a quarter of an avocado with two tablespoons of honey and an egg yolk. Spread it over your face (avoiding your eyes) and leave for about 15 minutes before rinsing with warm water.

Warning. Don't use any foods that you are allergic to.

HOW TO BE AN AUTOGRAPH HUNTER

It's great fun to collect autographs (signatures) from all your favourite celebs. You can put them together, store them beautifully, and show them off to all your friends. Here are some tops tips on how to be a successful autograph hunter.

▸ Buy or make a scrapbook or album for your autograph collection and decorate it however you want.

▸ Regularly check your local paper for events that celebrities will be attending, such as book signings or store openings, and ask someone to take you along. Be prepared to queue patiently for an autograph.

▸ If you spot a celebrity out and about and want to approach them for an autograph, always be polite. Only approach them if you feel it is appropriate – nobody likes being interrupted during a meal or in the middle of a phone call, for example.

Most celebrities love to meet their fans, so if you're polite and friendly, you're sure to get a good response from any celebrity you meet.

▶ Look up the addresses of fan clubs or celebrity agents, and write to them asking for an autograph. If you put some thought into your letter you will be more likely to get a reply. Tell them why you are a fan and a bit about yourself. Always include a stamped envelope with your address on it and a blank piece of paper for them to sign.

You will also love …

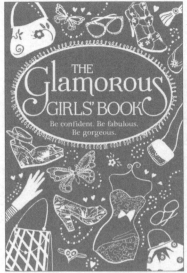

ISBN: 978-1-78055-020-6

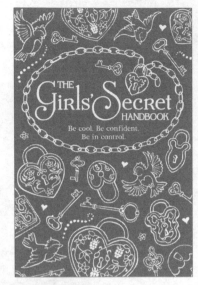

ISBN: 978-1-78055-180-7

ISBN: 978-1-78055-041-1